How to Succeed as a Substitute Teacher

This book is dedicated to all teachers and substitute teachers, for the important work that they do.

How to Succeed as a Substitute Teacher

Everything You Need From Start to Finish

Cicely Anne Rude

Corwin Press
A SAGE Company
Thousand Oaks, CA 91320

For information:

Corwin Press
A SAGE Company
2455 Teller Road
Thousand Oaks,
California 91320
www.corwinpress.com

SAGE India Pvt. Ltd.
B 1/I 1 Mohan Cooperative
Industrial Area
Mathura Road, New Delhi
India 110 044

SAGE Ltd.
1 Oliver's Yard
55 City Road
London EC1Y 1SP
United Kingdom

SAGE Asia-Pacific Pte. Ltd.
33 Pekin Street #02-01
Far East Square
Singapore 048763

Printed in the United States of America

Library of Congress Cataloging-in-Publication Data

Rude, Cicely Anne.
How to succeed as a substitute teacher : everything you need from start to finish/by Cicely Anne Rude.
p. cm.
Includes bibliographical references and index.
ISBN 978-1-4129-4474-8 (cloth)
ISBN 978-1-4129-4475-5 (pbk.)
1. Substitute teaching. 2. Substitute teachers. I. Title.

LB2844.1.S8R83 2008
371.1—dc22 2007020448

Printed on acid-free paper

07 08 09 10 11 12 13 10 9 8 7 6 5 4 3 2 1

Acquiring Editor: Carol Chambers Collins
Editorial Assistant: Gem Rabanera
Production Editor: Cassandra Margaret Seibel
Copy Editor: Sarah J. Duffy
Typesetter: C&M Digitals (P) Ltd.
Proofreader: Kevin Gleason
Indexer: Holly Day
Cover Designer: Monique Hahn
Graphic Designer: Lisa Riley

Contents

Foreword

No matter how long I teach, every August brings with it the same dream. It usually comes early in the month. I call it "the first-day-of-school dream."

It is simple. I'm in the front of a classroom as students I've never seen walk in. They look to me with the expectation that I'll get the class going. But I have no idea what to do, and I've prepared nothing. My anxiety builds as . . . .

I wake up with my heart racing, only to calm myself with the knowledge that the real first day is still a few weeks away. When that day arrives I am obsessively prepared, but my heart still races with nervousness. After all, teaching has many rewards and also many challenges, and to stand in front of a group of unknown students is nerve-racking, no matter how prepared we may be.

I can only imagine what it must be like to be a substitute teacher. The first-day nightmare could wake you up at any time of year. And as for nervously facing a new group of faces, that could be true five days a week.

In all the discussion about education in recent years, the role of the substitute is rarely addressed. The truth is, the substitute may be more important today than ever. In the current climate of high standards and high-stakes testing, every day matters. Students need to be regularly engaged in high-quality instruction, not just "kept busy" when the teacher is out. And teachers are out of class a great deal these days, typically to learn new ways to improve instruction. New teachers in support programs tend to miss even more days. If sub days are not valued, then imagine the horrible irony of students being pushed harder and harder—except on the many occasions when the teacher is not around.

In this new paradigm, a substitute needs to be respected as an educator. That is easy to say but not so easy to realize when the same person may need to teach biology one day, French the next, and reading to special education fifth graders after that. I don't expect substitutes to have a master's degree in my subject, but I do expect them to carefully read and follow directions. Unfortunately, substitutes need to be much more resourceful than that. After all, directions from teachers can be vague, insufficient, or at worst, nonexistent.

Imagine this scenario. A substitute shows up on time but is delayed in the hectic main office and makes it to the classroom at the last minute only to discover no plans. As terrible as that sounds, a well-prepared substitute will have something in the bag—probably literally. Additionally, the well-prepared substitute will know how to exude confidence despite the anxiety that is not far from the surface.

Becoming well prepared can take time, possibly years. This book offers an attractive shortcut. Cicely Rude, who has worked as both a substitute and a teacher, is a talented writer with a keen sense of observation. This book goes a long way toward offering solutions so that a day with a substitute need not be a day without education, and the night before need not be restless.

—Donald Bott
Journalism Teacher
Amos Alonzo Stagg High School
Stockton, California

Preface

A Message to All Substitute Teachers

I want you to let your mind wander back, for just a moment, to your primary or secondary school days. Can you think of a substitute teacher in your past who could have made an hour or a day more enjoyable and productive for both him- or herself and for you? If you are like most Americans, you can remember at least a few substitutes who tried to fill your teachers' shoes. Some were probably entertaining, some humorless, some too strict, and some easy to walk all over. Some were probably more effective educators than others. Substitute teaching can be a difficult job to do well, but it doesn't have to be, thanks to this book, *How to Succeed as a Substitute Teacher: Everything You Need From Start to Finish.*

In 1997, I abandoned a career in retail management to answer the "calling to teach," as Herbert Kohl (1984) puts it. No, nobody called me on the phone and said, "Hey Cicely! You should be a teacher!" Teaching was simply something that I discovered I needed to do. Today, I am a professor of education. However, I began my career in education as a nervous substitute teacher in a public school district, frantically prowling the local bookstores and public library for a helpful "how to" book that I never found. What you are now holding in your hands is the book that I *wish* I'd had when I began substitute teaching. It provides substitutes with the tools that they need to serve effectively in the many classrooms where they are needed.

While a graduate student studying education, I used substitute teaching to explore teaching options; interact with students, teachers, administrators, and other subs; practice the art of classroom management; and earn some money. I subbed in many different schools and programs, including elementary, secondary, adult, bilingual, and alternative education. I also conducted informational interviews with teachers and substitute teachers, chatted with students and staff, and observed classes. For two years, I took notes on all my experiences as a sub. Those notes included information about applying for work in a school district, arriving at a school for the first time, working with teachers, managing student behavior, tapping into sources of student motivation, and more. The resulting book is therefore based on a combination of qualitative research and practical experience. It provides useful information punctuated by anecdotes of my own experiences and those of other subs, real-world examples, and a few tidbits of timeless wisdom.

I have designed this book specifically to offer practical, hands-on advice to all substitute teachers. Whether you have decided to work as a sub temporarily before moving on to another career, are considering earning a teaching credential, or plan to make substitute teaching your profession, this book can help. I offer you, the reader, everything you need to know about finding information about subbing in your state or district, the types of work opportunities available to you, common school procedures, classroom management, basic lesson planning, and safety. Best of all, the book includes eight classroom management tips that I developed *specifically* for use by short-term substitutes to make the job as low stress and enjoyable as possible.

Here is what each chapter has to offer:

Chapter 1 briefly discusses why substitute teachers are so vital to our education system and then moves on to some of the opportunities and variations that are poised to present themselves to you as a sub.

Chapters 2 and 3 are about walking onto a school campus to sub for the first time and being professional, responsible, and reliable. They include sample schedules, basic responsibilities and pertinent legal issues, lists of useful materials to have on hand, and lists of things to do before, during, and after class.

Chapter 4 goes further to help you make the most of your position in the school system by networking, developing professional relationships with faculty and administrators, and learning from your own experiences as a student.

Chapter 5 is the heart of this book, with eight classroom management tips specifically designed for use by short-term subs who don't have months or even days to gradually get to know the students and establish patterns of behavior.

Chapter 6 is a brief explanation of simple precautionary steps that you can take as a sub to ensure the safety of yourself, your students, your personal belongings, and the school buildings and property. After all, an ounce of prevention is worth a pound of cure.

I am thrilled that I have the opportunity to share the wealth of practical information in this book with new substitute teachers. If you read it, apply it to your work, and add your own expertise and experiences, you will be far better-equipped to succeed than I was at the start of my educational career!

Acknowledgments

I would like to thank the following people for helping to bring this book to life: Rosalind, Leland, and Robin Rude, and the rest of my ever-supportive family; Michael Stone for never failing to be a supportive husband; Rocky and Gretchen Stone for their ongoing assistance; and Andrea Alvillar, Don Bott, and other teachers for helping to develop my interests in teaching and writing over the years. I would also like to thank my students, colleagues, and the Corwin Press editorial staff for their invaluable input and support.

Corwin Press thanks the following reviewers for their contribution to this book:

Melody L. Aldrich
English Teacher
Florence High School
Florence, AZ

Ed Aust
Adult ESL Teacher and
Substitute Teacher
Oakland, CA

Carol Aymar
Teacher
Francis W. Parker School
Chicago, IL

Deanna Brunlinger
Science Teacher, NBCT
Elkhorn Area High School
Elkhorn, WI

Kellie Cain
Assistant Professor,
Curriculum and Instruction
Benerd School of Education
University of the Pacific
Stockton, CA

Carrie Carpenter
Program Coordinator
Deschutes Edge Charter School
Oregon Teacher of the Year 2003
Redmond, OR

Elizabeth F. Day
Teacher
Mechanicville Middle School
New York State 2005 Teacher
of the Year
Mechanicville, NY

Jolene Dockstader
Seventh-Grade English Teacher
Jerome School District #261
Jerome, ID

Roxie Fussell
NBCT of Pre-K ESE
Lake County School Board
Leesburg, FL

Ann Go
Assistant Professor
Department of Curriculum and Instruction
Benerd School of Education
University of the Pacific
Stockton, CA

Florence Krokos
Teacher
Harding Elementary
Granada Hills, CA

Michelle Nangin-Woods
Educational Consultant
Albany, CA

Robert Oprandy
Professor of Education
University of the Pacific
Benerd School of Education
Stockton, CA

Adrienne Reck
NBCT
Eagles Landing Middle School
Boca Raton, FL

Rebecca Sauer
Math Teacher
South High School
Denver, CO

Claudia Schwartz
Director of Field Experiences
Benerd School of Education
University of the Pacific
Stockton, CA

Beverly Wixon
Language Arts Department Chair
Kathleen Middle School
Lakeland, FL

About the Author

Cicely Anne Rude teaches in the Benerd School of Education at the University of the Pacific in Stockton, California. Ms. Rude specializes in teaching courses about language learning and teaching for undergraduate and graduate students who are pursuing California teacher credentials. She earned her master's degree in teaching English to speakers of other languages (TESOL) at the Monterey Institute of International Studies. In addition to working as a public school substitute teacher for two years, her diverse experiences include teaching English in Japan, teaching adult English as a second language, and teaching linguistics.

As the author of numerous newspaper and academic journal articles on the subject of education, as well as resource materials for teachers, Ms. Rude has developed teacher education workshops for organizations including California Teachers of English to Speakers of Other Languages (CATESOL), the Japan Exchange and Teaching (JET) Program, and the Consulate General of Japan in San Francisco.

Introduction

WHY SUBSTITUTE TEACHERS ARE IMPORTANT

Short-term and long-term substitute teachers are in constant demand, and they play a key role in ensuring that our public education system continues to function. The National Education Association (2006) defines substitute teachers in the following way:

> Substitute educators perform a vital function in the maintenance and continuity of daily education. In our public school systems, substitutes are the educational bridges when regular classroom educators are absent. They are called early in the morning, take over lessons with short notice, and ensure that quality education is maintained in our classrooms. The professional substitute ensures that time is productive and furthers the student's learning. (¶ 1)

Without subs, our public school system would come to a grinding halt. For example, according to the National Education Association (2005), there were 3,105,783 teachers working in the United States in the 2004–2005 school year. Geoffrey Smith, director of the Substitute Teaching Institute at Utah State University, estimates that 8% to 10% of teachers are absent on any given school day; most of these absences are due to professional development meetings, workshops, and classes. Therefore, it is possible that as many as 310,578 substitute teachers are needed each day. In fact, approximately one full year of a student's K–12 education is taught by substitute teachers (Substitute Teaching Institute 2007).

Across the nation, as long as teachers are human beings who occasionally get sick, attend conferences or professional development workshops, deal with personal emergencies, and have car trouble, there should be ample need for your services as a substitute teacher.

HOW DO YOU DEFINE SUCCESS?

Before walking into a classroom, I suggest that you take a few moments to think about these three questions:

1. Why are you substitute teaching?
2. What do you hope to gain from subbing?
3. What do you hope to contribute as a sub?

These are important questions, because if you can articulate exactly why you are substitute teaching and what you hope to gain in terms of experience, education, finances, career, and so on, then you have defined what *success* means to you. Additionally, you can increase your chances of successfully meeting your goals and feeling good about your work.

While working in public school districts, I have sat in many different teachers' lounges and met many subs. Chatting with them, I quickly discovered that each had a reason for what he or she was doing. For example, recent college graduates sometimes work as subs while searching for a full-time job, or they do it because they are temporarily unsure of the career path they wish to pursue. Occasionally, people who are between jobs or are in the process of changing careers sub for a while. Many retired teachers and other professionals also serve as subs. And of course, there are also those who use substitute teaching to fund graduate studies and/or gain experience working in various types of public school classroom environments.

I chose to substitute teach because it was a convenient way to gain classroom experience in a wide variety of settings and earn money while attending graduate school. However, my reasons for subbing certainly don't apply to everyone. My most lively conversation on the subject of why people substitute teach was with a young man who had resigned from his job as an attorney to teach elementary school and was serving as a long-term sub until his teaching license came through. We chatted on a playground during recess one day. He was very excited about his new career and had built a great rapport with his students. Here are some other reasons that people have given me; subs have told me that they

- Enjoy the freedom of not being tied down to one school or one class.
- Retired from teaching but missed working and now sub a few days each week.
- Think they might like to get a teaching credential/license but aren't yet sure.
- Just graduated from college and need to earn some money while searching for a regular job in another field.
- Are looking for a full-time teaching position and subbing in the meantime.

So back to the question of why *you* are subbing. When you have your answer(s) ready, write them in the space below, and refer back to them now and again to make sure that you are meeting your own goals and getting the satisfaction you need from your job.

I am subbing because . . .

____

____

____

I hope to gain . . .

____

____

____

I hope to contribute . . .

____

____

____

Chapter One

Welcome to Substitute Teaching!

I can't emphasize enough that a substitute teacher plays a vital role in the field of education. When a regular teacher is absent from school, a substitute steps into the breach, sometimes at very short notice, and prevents the learning process from coming to a stop. Subbing is both an important and a challenging job that is full of variety. This first chapter introduces you to the many sources of variety that you may experience as a substitute teacher and discusses some potential benefits and drawbacks of this line of work.

DIFFERENT WORK OPPORTUNITIES THAT MAY BE AVAILABLE TO YOU

Variety is a word that lends itself perfectly well to describing the world of substitute teaching. To begin with, jobs last for different lengths of time. A teacher may require a substitute for half a day, a whole school day, several days, a week, or more. Lengthy jobs are commonly referred to as *long-term substitute* positions or *extended-term assignments,* but your school district may have a different name for them. Different districts define long-term substitute teaching assignments in slightly different ways, but they usually require the sub to cover all of an absent teacher's duties for more than 15 days, give or take. Long-term subs are usually paid more than short-term subs and are often required to meet different qualification standards, which vary by state.

In addition to different time frames, most substitute teachers have the opportunity to work with students at different grade levels, teach different subjects, experience different scheduling arrangements, and involve themselves in different types of school programs. As a short-term sub, you may be subject to restrictions regarding which grades and subject matter you are qualified to teach. On the other hand, as a long-term sub, you may find yourself working with the same group of students for many days or many months. Nevertheless, while subbing, you will most likely have opportunities to work in a variety of classroom environments.

Types of Schools

When a sub signs up with a school district, he or she usually has the option of working in almost any school within that district, and this alone offers many possibilities. To make things even better, as a substitute, you may be able to simultaneously sign up with and work in as many public school districts as you like—or at least as many as you can commute to. Across the United States, some schools hire full-time subs to work regularly at one location, but these jobs are comparatively few. Different types of schools vary with the location and size of school districts, and a large district is likely to have more opportunities than a smaller one (although this is not always the case). Below are the types of schools in which substitute teachers most commonly have the option of working, along with a brief explanation of each

Primary School

These schools usually serve Kindergarten through Grade 3. As the substitute teacher, you usually stay with the same students all day, teaching all their subjects. You might be needed to help supervise the playground during recess time or the cafeteria during lunchtime. Young students often have nap and/or snack time built into their schedules.

Elementary School

These schools usually serve Kindergarten through Grade 6, although some schools may include Grades 7 and 8 and are more aptly called *K–8 schools*. As in primary schools, you usually stay with the same students all day, teaching all their subjects, and you might be needed to help supervise the playground during recess time or the cafeteria during lunchtime.

Junior High/Middle School

These schools usually serve students in Grades 7 and 8, but sometimes include Grade 9. Schedules tend to be similar to a high school format, with students moving from one classroom to the next for each subject.

K–8 School

Some public school districts have schools for Kindergarten through eighth grade, eliminating the need for junior high or middle schools. Also, many private schools are attended by students through the eighth grade.

High School

These schools generally include Grades 9 through 12, or sometimes 10 through 12. If you sub for a high school teacher, you will probably stay in one classroom, while a new group of students joins you for each class period. If you choose to sub at the high school level, your district may ask you to indicate what subject matter (e.g., English, math, French, physical education) you are comfortable with and qualified to teach.

Continuation High School

These are schools for students who have dropped out of or been expelled from a regular high school in the district. Often, this is their last opportunity to earn a high school diploma.

Youth Authority

Some teachers (and therefore substitute teachers, too) teach students in juvenile detention centers. Guards are usually present or nearby. Teachers and substitutes usually get paid more for working in a youth authority than for working in a regular school.

School for Adults

Schools for adults are not the same as alternative high schools, although many offer classes through which young adults can earn a high school diploma or GED certificate. They also offer English as a second language (ESL) and citizenship classes for adult immigrants, parenting classes, computer training, and more for members of the community. Some serve as centers for community education. Each is part of a school district, and many use substitute teachers.

Newcomer School

These are schools dedicated to serving the needs of learners who have recently immigrated to the United States and are acclimatizing socially and learning to use English.

Department of Defense Dependents' School

Schools on American military bases are overseen by the Department of Defense Education Activity (DoDEA). Sometimes referred to as *Federal Schools*, DoDEA's schools serve the children of military service members and Department of Defense civilian employees throughout the world. DoDEA operates public schools in the United States and overseas.

Types of Programs

The schools at which you substitute teach will probably have a variety of different programs to serve the needs of their student populations. Below are just some of the more common programs in which you may have opportunities to substitute teach.

Bilingual Education

Bilingual education programs appear at all education levels. The word *bilingual* is of Latin origin. *Bi* means two, and *lingua* is the root word for tongue or language. Hence, one of the goals of bilingual education is for students to become proficient in two languages. There are different types of bilingual education programs with different instructional approaches, including but not limited to English Language Development (ELD) and Special Designed Academic Instruction in English (SDAIE). Such programs are designed to provide limited-English-proficient (LEP) students with temporary assistance as they learn to function in an English-speaking academic environment. Some classes are contained, meaning that the students remain in the same class all day. Others are in pullout programs, wherein the students leave their regular classes and attend for only part of the school day. Paraprofessionals are often present to assist in these classes.

ESL

ESL programs are designed specifically to teach English to LEP students, and these programs appear at all levels of education. Many school districts offer ESL classes for adult learners. There are many different types of ESL classes, including but not limited to English for academic purposes (EAP), Survival English (or English for use in day-to-day tasks such as communicating with a doctor), adult literacy (to help parents read to their children), civics or citizenship (for adults who wish to become U.S. citizens), and more.

Special Education

Special education is a very broad term, but these programs basically exist to help students who have disabilities that are not always accommodated in mainstream classrooms. Disabilities may include autism, blindness, deafness, emotional disorders, learning disabilities, mental retardation (also known as cognitive impairment or intellectual disability), orthopedic impairments, speech or language impairments, and traumatic brain injury. Special education teachers are trained to work specifically with students who have exceptional needs and are often assisted by paraprofessionals. Schools have different ways of meeting the needs of special education students, but here are a few common support methods (*Substitute Teacher Handbook K–12* 2004):

- A general education classroom in which a few students with special needs spend all or part of the school day in the classroom, possibly accompanied by paraprofessionals
- A pullout program in which students leave their classrooms and spend part of the school day in a resource room
- Several general education classrooms, through which a special education teacher moves, coteaching with other teachers.
- A self-contained classroom in which students with similar disabilities spend most or all of the school day

Gifted and Talented Education (GATE)

Students who perform above average are often invited to participate in either a pullout program (one or two hours per day) or contained classes for gifted learners. Gifted and talented students usually demonstrate above-average academic ability, have a high level of task commitment, and are very creative. All variations of GATE programs strive to provide intellectually stimulating learning environments for participating students. The Substitute Teaching Institute at Utah State University's *Substitute Teacher Handbook K–12* (2004) recommends several key *do's* and *don'ts* to keep in mind when working with gifted and talented students:

Do . . .

- Use enrichment and extension activities
- Use puzzles and games
- Assign alternative projects (such as collages and posters)
- Use comparisons and analogies

Don't . . .

- Make them repeat tasks they have already mastered
- Make them always work with slower students
- Have them memorize, recite, and copy just to fill time

Your local school district might not have all of the schools and programs described in this chapter. Alternately, it may offer an even wider variety of opportunities. If you have decided to use your job as a substitute teacher as a means of determining (a) if you want to earn a teaching license and (b) the sort of environment in which you want to teach, I strongly recommend working with students at all age levels and in as many different types of schools and programs as are available to you. Incidentally, it was through substitute teaching various high school bilingual classes and adult ESL classes that I first grew interested in teaching ESL to adult learners.

Up to this point, I have been talking about public school districts, but I would like to mention the option of subbing at private schools as well. I tend to emphasize substitute teaching in public schools because many subs can sign up to work in all of the schools in a district with just one application. If you are facing a substantial amount of paperwork to be approved as a substitute by the state and then hired by a district, this can be a welcome convenience. Private schools will often maintain their own substitute teacher pools, and you might have to contact each school that you wish to work for individually. Some private schools contract with employment agencies for their substitute teachers, so you might contact one in your area and ask if it contracts with any local private schools. However, if you live near a private school where you would like to substitute teach now and again, or if you have previously been involved with a private school as an alumnus, a parent, or a former instructor, contact the school officials to inquire about substitute teaching possibilities and hiring procedures.

VARIATIONS IN SCHEDULING

The final variation that I mention is that of scheduling—for the school year as well as for the school day. Different schools have different schedules. Some follow a traditional school year, late August through early June, with summer, winter, and spring vacations. Others are year-round schools that do not follow the traditional school year. In a year-round school, different students have short breaks at different times of the year. Scheduling at the school(s) where you work as a substitute teacher may differ from what you experienced as an elementary or secondary school student.

Not only do schools begin and end at different times during the day, but some secondary schools utilize block schedules as opposed to traditional daily schedules. A junior high or high school operating on a traditional schedule will have about six to eight class periods per day, of about 55 minutes each, with a lunch break that usually falls between the fourth and fifth periods. Some large schools have multiple lunch breaks, and each student is assigned to one of them. Some schools even have staggered schedules, in which case there are more than six or seven periods per day. In this case, half of the students in the school might arrive and leave an hour earlier, attending periods one through seven, whereas the other half arrive and leave an hour later, attending periods two through eight. High schools generally have longer days than elementary schools do. In a more exaggerated version of the staggered schedule, some students attend from about 7:30 a.m. until 2:00 p.m., other students attend from about 11:00 a.m. until 5:00 p.m., and the teachers work either the morning or afternoon shift. As a substitute, be sure that you know what time you are expected to begin work at a particular school.

In one example of a block schedule, students attend all of their classes on Mondays for about 55 minutes each, as on a traditional schedule. On Tuesdays and Thursdays they attend the classes that they are assigned to for periods one, three, and five for about one hour and 50 minutes each, with a break of 20 minutes after the first class and then a lunch break after the second class. Then, on Wednesday and Fridays, they attend periods two, four, and six. The result is that classes are longer and may be more involved, and substitutes need to pay close attention to the day of the week before beginning to read names off the attendance sheets. Chapter 3 contains some examples of school schedules.

I should mention that secondary school teachers usually have one empty (no scheduled class) period in their schedule that is reserved for preparation. This *prep period* occurs every day on a traditional schedule. On a block schedule, it occurs only three days per week, but for two hours at a time. As a result, a sub who fills in for a particular teacher for only one day at a high school with a block schedule might work for about six hours with no prep period or for only four hours and rest for two, depending on the day of the week. Some subs may be asked to help out in other ways (e.g., filling in for other teachers, assisting in the office) during a prep period, whereas others may not. Subs in some areas get paid the same amount for the day, regardless, which brings me to the next topic of discussion: average pay.

AVERAGE PAY

Over $2 billion is spent annually on substitute teacher pay in the United States (Substitute Teaching Institute 2007). I want to preface this section by pointing out that substitute teacher pay rates vary widely across states and school districts. Moreover, pay in many areas increases each year or so. Your local school or district is your best source of up-to-date information regarding how much you can expect to be paid as a sub, but I can offer some averages, ballpark figures, and relevant variables. Resource A, at the end of this book, contains contact information for the agency in charge of public education in each state, and your local public and private schools can be found in the white pages of a telephone directory. Also, more and more schools and school districts are developing their own Web pages.

When I first tried my hand at substitute teaching back in 1997, I signed up with two school districts that were both located within five miles of each other in Northern California. One paid $110 per day, and the other paid $85 per day. Pay rates tend to vary depending on the geographic area, the school district, and the length of the substitute teaching assignment. In a few states, substitute teacher pay increases with the sub's level of education. However, most school districts offer a set daily rate for all subs, only paying more to those with full teaching licenses.

I can't list the pay scales for different districts in this chapter because that sort of information can change too rapidly to remain accurate for long. However, school district offices disclose their pay rates for substitute teachers in their application materials and/or online. If you have yet to make employment arrangements with a school or district, I suggest calling those in your area and asking what they offer. School district main offices are generally listed in the local telephone directory. Alternately, as I mentioned before, contact information for state departments of education can be found in Resource A.

Meanwhile, here are a few examples of what sort of daily pay some subs have earned. The average substitute teacher pay in the United States was $65 per day in 2003 (National Substitute Teachers Alliance 2003). In 2006, the Oregon School Boards Association (2006) advertised a minimum substitute teacher daily pay rate of $139.17. At the same time, New York City offered substitute teachers $140.14 per day (NYC Department of Education 2006). In Idaho, pay rates ranged from about $50 to $75 per day for the 2006–2007 school year (Boise School District Employment and Application Center 2006). New subs are fingerprinted, and their backgrounds are checked before they can begin working. Some school districts cover the expense of this process, but others do not.

For the purpose of comparison across areas, here are a few sample average reported pay rates for subs from 2002 (National Substitute Teacher Alliance 2003):

Table 1.1 Samples of Average Pay Rates

School District	*Pay Per Day in 2002*
Los Angeles, CA	$152
Omaha, NE	$140
New York, NY	$128
Minneapolis, MN	$121
Chicago, IL	$104

Aside from the day-to-day work that substitutes do, they are often met with opportunities to engage in long-term assignments. Subs who stay in the same assignment for an extended period of time, often 15 days or more but variable by area, earn a higher daily pay rate than subs in short-term assignments.

Some assignments are paid hourly rather than daily. These can include, but are not necessarily exclusive to, special education and evening adult ESL classes. Check with your school or district to find out exactly which substitute teaching assignments, if any, pay by the hour.

PROS AND CONS

Anyone who has spent time as a substitute teacher has probably recognized that the job has some distinct advantages over others, as well as some disadvantages. I'm going to let you know what the common advantages and disadvantages are, as discovered by myself and subs I met in my travels from school to school.

The Good!

Most subs enjoy the luxury of comparatively short workdays. At some schools, I was able to cover all of a teacher's classes for the day in four or five hours (he or she had a prep period in the afternoon) and was sent home in time for a late lunch. However, please note that some schools require substitutes to remain on campus for the entire school day, regardless of the class schedule. If you arrive on campus and discover that you are subbing for a teacher whose day ends with an afternoon prep period, I strongly suggest asking the principal about the school policy regarding substitutes' time at work before you head home, so as not to put your job in jeopardy. Most regular teachers arrive on campus early and stay late to make preparations, plan lessons, read and write feedback on papers, grade exams, and supervise activities. Short-term substitutes usually don't engage in any of those activities. As a result, even on days when they have to teach every class period, substitutes can arrive on campus only about 15 or 20 minutes before classes begin and leave shortly after they end. That usually results in a working day of roughly six hours, with a lunch break of roughly half an hour, give or take. That's not a bad schedule, especially for a sub who has a second job or is taking college courses.

The wide variety of different experiences available to substitute teachers is another major advantage of this job. When I began subbing, I had a vague idea that I wanted to teach, but I wanted to know more about classroom environments and the different options available to me before I enrolled in a teacher credentialing program and wrote a check for my first tuition payment. Substitute teaching in a public school district offers the opportunity to gain experience in many different types of classroom situations in a relatively short amount of time. This variety can be highly beneficial for subs who are considering teaching as a profession or who have decided to become teachers but are not yet sure of what age level and/or subject matter they prefer. Also, for subs who are not planning to become credentialed teachers, the variety can make every day interesting.

Yet another benefit of the job is the potential for networking and developing professional contacts. Whether you are subbing for a short time, are planning to do it for many years, or would like to earn a credential and become a full-time regular teacher, subbing is an excellent means of meeting school faculty and administrators and demonstrating your abilities. Networking and proving yourself to be dependable can make you a much-sought-after substitute. Additionally, a sub who plans to become a licensed teacher can use networking to find a desirable student teaching position.

I mention the possibility of using substitute teaching to explore possible student teaching opportunities because subs sometimes discover that they would like to enroll in teacher education courses and become licensed teachers. The teacher-licensing process often includes student teaching, which can sometimes be replaced by time spent working as an intern. Student teachers work under the guidance of a master teacher and share his or her classroom for a semester. They are unpaid. Interns are full-time teachers who teach their own classes, are paid less than their credentialed colleagues, are frequently hired by schools that can't find enough credentialed teachers to cover all of the classes, and receive credit from their university or credentialing program. Building connections, strong working relationships, and a reputation as a reliable substitute can lead to an easier time getting hired as an intern or a permanent teacher. For credential candidates who prefer to student teach rather than intern, subbing is a good opportunity to meet teachers and students and to decide where a preferable student teaching experience might be found.

Finally, most substitute teachers have a great deal of autonomy regarding their work schedules. By autonomy, I mean that most subs have the freedom to choose which days they work and which they don't (full-time substitutes excluded). Most subs can also decide which schools, grade levels, and programs in the district they want to work at and which ones they don't feel comfortable with. Of course, your own freedom of choice in this respect might be restricted by your budget, and if you don't work, you don't get paid. Please bear in mind that refusing a job may damage your chances of being offered another right away, and that the amount of freedom you have to pick and choose your substitute teaching assignments will naturally depend on local factors, including your school or district's demand for subs and policies regarding substitute teachers.

The Not-So-Good

Of course, subbing is not a perfect job. Whether you choose to do it for six months or six years, some difficulties are bound to surface. Substitute teachers have three key disadvantages compared to full-time teachers. First, there is the issue of medical insurance.

Today, most Americans who have medical insurance get it through their jobs as part of a benefits package. I have yet to find a school district that offers a comprehensive benefits package to its part-time substitute teachers. Fortunately, substitutes are eligible (and sometimes required) to join a local teachers union, and some of those unions negotiate discounted rates with local doctors and dentists for their members.

The next problem is consistency, or rather the lack thereof. A substitute teacher can work in a different classroom every day of the month. Granted, as a sub, you will probably be offered some two- and three-day assignments. I once filled in for the same math teacher for almost two weeks and I must admit that having a routine was a refreshing change. It can be stressful for some people to walk into a different classroom and size up a new group of students every day. For others, the variety can be invigorating.

Finally, each school is different, but as a substitute teacher you might find that you don't have a well-defined place in the school or district hierarchy. Subs are not full-time teachers. They have neither the pay, nor the benefits, nor the long-term authority that regular teachers have, and students are usually aware of that. As a sub who is only filling in for a day or even half a day, you can't realistically threaten to lower a disruptive student's grades. Fortunately, I have subbed in many schools where my presence was appreciated by faculty, staff, and students who recognized the important role that substitutes play. As for any disruptive students, the strategies in Chapter 5 can make them easier to work with than they might otherwise be.

TIPS TO TAKE WITH YOU

- Subs often have opportunities to teach in many different types of schools, programs, grade levels, and schedules. Check with your school or district to find out which may be available to you.
- Substitute teacher pay varies widely and is subject to change. Ask your district office about current pay rates, or contact one of the state departments of education listed in Resource A.

FOOD FOR THOUGHT

Ask yourself the questions below. If you can't answer them, ask someone at your school or district office. Finding answers will help you mentally prepare and learn about the lay of the land, so to speak, before starting out as a new sub or subbing in a new school or district.

1. What types of schools are in your district, unit, or area? At how many and which of those schools are you both qualified and interested in subbing? Why?

____

____

____

____

____

2. In your opinion, what are the good and not-so-good aspects of subbing at each? How might you focus on the good points and reduce or negate the not-so-good points?

____

____

____

____

____

3. Do you plan to be selective about your substitute teaching assignments? How and why? Do you have the option of not accepting an assignment?

Chapter Two

Setting Sail as a Sub

I have met many people who have expressed interest in substitute teaching, and who are highly qualified, but have never pursued that interest because they didn't know where to begin. I have also met new subs who have walked into their first assignment with little or no preparation. Therefore, the goals of this chapter are twofold. The first is to point prospective subs toward key sources of information regarding how to apply for a substitute teaching position. The second is to help new subs begin to prepare for that first day at work on a school campus.

Requirements for substitute teachers vary from one state to another, and often from one school district to another, or even between schools. As I write this chapter, minimum requirements for subs range from being a high school graduate to completing a bachelor's degree and teacher training coursework. Many states, including California and Colorado, require substitute teachers to pass a basic skills test. Many require substitute teachers to have completed a bachelor's degree. And some require specific certification for subs, whereas others leave the matter in the hands of the districts or individual schools. In any case, the world of education is always changing, and your state office of education should be able to tell you how to proceed toward subbing in your state. Prospective substitutes should contact a school district's main office to determine current state and local requirements and to begin the process of applying for a permit to substitute teach, if a state-granted permit is necessary. Contact information for your local school district's main administrative office should be listed in your local phone book. Information on how to contact the department responsible for licensing public school educators in each state, as well as minimum requirements for subs, can be found in Resource A at the end of this book.

GETTING STARTED IN YOUR NEW JOB

If you have been hired as a substitute teacher and are ready to accept your first assignment, then please accept my congratulations! I want to take this opportunity to remind you that the role you are undertaking is an important one, and you are a valuable member of a community of educators. If you have been hired by a school district (or unit), as opposed to a single school, there are some important pieces of information that you should be sure to obtain from the district office *before* walking into your first substitute teaching assignment. This information may be prepared in advance by your employer and simply handed to you. However, if that doesn't happen, I recommend asking for the information or making an effort to collect it yourself. Use the list below to make sure that you get what you need. The items on this list might seem like obvious necessities, but I highlight them here because obvious things can easily get overlooked, especially by people who are busy. Therefore, be sure to obtain (or be certain that you don't need) the following:

- The names of the schools in the district (or those at which you are eligible to work, in case of any restrictions)
- The student grade levels and/or special programs taught at each school (e.g., elementary, middle, high, combined, alternative, adult, other)
- The street address for each school site (maps and/or directions are an added help if you are not familiar with the area, but you can compile these yourself if necessary)
- Start and dismissal times for each school
- The time(s) at which subs are expected to arrive at each school and what time they may leave
- District and school office telephone numbers

- Salary schedule, payment procedures, and necessary documents (so that your paycheck is not delayed due to incorrect paperwork)
- Information about teachers' union membership. Are you eligible and/or required to join? What costs and benefits apply to you as a substitute teacher?

PARKING

Your arrival at school can set the tone for the rest of your workday. When I accepted my first substitute teaching assignment, I had a lot of things on my mind. After all, I was very young and about to step onto a high school campus as an authority figure, and not as a student, for the first time. I remembered to bring my time card (after all, I needed to get paid), but I overlooked the simple matter of parking. Later, through chatting with other subs in various teachers' lounges, I discovered that I was not the only sub to arrive at a school site for the first time and then wonder where to leave my car. Not knowing where to park is a comparatively small problem, but it can start your morning off on the wrong foot, so to speak. Teacher parking is not always clearly marked, nor is it always separated from student parking (in the case of some high school campuses). Also, some parking lots can be closed at certain times during the day. Finally, school mailing addresses and street addresses do not always match.

Therefore, save yourself a bit of a hassle. If you plan to drive to a school and haven't been to that campus before, consider calling the school's main office in advance, introducing yourself as a new sub, and asking where to park.

AT THE SCHOOL SITE: INFORMATION AND MATERIAL TO LOOK FOR UPON ARRIVAL

With your car safely stowed, your first stop should be the school's main office. A secretary or receptionist is usually entrusted with the task of greeting substitute teachers and handing out necessary information and materials. When you report for work, try to get (or establish that you don't need) the following information and materials:

Forms and/or instructions for reporting student attendance

Attendance forms, sometimes called *roll sheets*, that have the name of each student in your class(es). If you are subbing in a secondary school, check to see if you have one list per class. At some high schools, attendance may be reported electronically. This may be done either via computer or telephone. If such is the case at one of your schools, ask how to do it and find out if you need a password.

The subject (e.g., math, science, art) or grade level that you will be in charge of for the day

The room number and location of your classroom

To my utter delight, a small elementary school used to have a student proudly escort me to my classroom in the morning. The school was too small to get lost in, but the service made me feel very welcome and gave the day a lovely beginning. As a sub, I hope that you can collect some happy memories of your own.

A map of the campus

This might not be necessary at small schools, but it can be very useful at big schools or those that have been added onto with many temporary or portable buildings.

A timetable

This should include either start and dismissal times for each period at junior high and high schools or start, dismissal, lunch, and recess times at elementary schools. Be sure to check if you are responsible for supervising students at lunch and/or recess time.

The regular teacher's notes and instructions

Except in unusual cases, you should be presented with a lesson plan and materials to use. These might be left in the classroom on the teacher's desk if the office doesn't have them. Many schools require teachers to prepare "emergency" lesson plans that are ready for a sub to use in case of an unexpected absence. For more information about how you can prepare for those occasions when a lesson plan is not provided, please refer to Chapter 3.

Basic school policies regarding student discipline

Find out in advance what procedure has been established for sending particularly unruly students out of your classroom, and how to use it. You may also request a copy of the Safe Schools Policy. Hopefully, with the help of Chapter 5, you won't have to resort to extreme disciplinary measures very often. Nevertheless, you should always be prepared.

An emergency evacuation map

You will need to know where to lead your students in case of a fire drill or an actual fire. This information may be posted inside the classroom. I participated in a couple of fire drills while subbing, and it's possible that you will, too.

SUBSTITUTE TEACHER RESPONSIBILITIES

At this point I would like to mention what are generally regarded as a substitute teacher's responsibilities (Chapter 3 goes on to provide a general procedural guide):

- Follow the regular teacher's prepared lesson plan (but have an emergency backup plan ready, and notify someone if a plan has not been left).
- Instruct students.
- Assign lessons as necessary or as requested by the regular teacher.
- Maintain accurate attendance records.
- Perform any special duties that are assigned (e.g., monitoring the lunchroom, hallways, or playground).
- Take care of the classroom and all property that is in your charge for the duration of your sub assignment.
- Apprise the regular teacher of what took place and what material was covered during his or her absence.
- Supervise students, maintaining discipline and safety at all times. The next section on legal issues further explains this final responsibility.

Legal Issues

Your school or district should provide you with information regarding your specific responsibilities and legal obligations as a substitute teacher. However, here are eight points that are fairly universal (several of which are elaborated upon in Chapter 6):

1. You are responsible for supervising your students and ensuring that their conduct is orderly and safe. In many states, teachers act in *loco parentis* (in lieu of a parent), so use your best judgment to ensure the safety of your students and the progression of their education. Never leave your students without adult supervision.

2. Exercise due care and caution for the safety of the students in your care. Follow all school safety policies and procedures.

3. Do not allow your students to leave school property without express permission from the office.

4. Never give any medication to a student. This includes over-the-counter painkillers. Only the school nurse or other authorized health personnel should give medication to a student.

5. Do not disclose confidential information about students. Refrain from discussing their grades, medical conditions, learning disabilities, and so on.

6. Learn your state and school policies on student discipline, and uphold them. Ensure that your students' learning environment is safe. Watch for potential hazards, obstructed exits, and so on. If the lesson plan instructs you to conduct an activity with which you are uncomfortable, you may choose to do an alternate activity that you believe to be safer.

7. If you have reason to suspect a case of child abuse, sexual abuse, or neglect, report it immediately to the school principal or a peace officer (*Substitute Teacher Handbook K–12* 2004).

8. Some teachers advocate the use of candy as an incentive for good student behavior. Please refrain from giving any candy or snacks to your students. As a sub, you most likely will not know which students are on special diets, which

have dangerous food allergies, and so on. For example, some children are highly allergic to peanuts, even in trace amounts, and can die from a piece of candy or cookie prepared in a factory that also processes peanuts. Read the next section on substitute teacher supplies for some effective (and nonedible) alternative incentives.

SUBSTITUTE TEACHER SUPPLIES

A well-prepared substitute carries a few supplies to school, just in case they are needed. Sometimes called a *sub pack,* these supplies can help you be professional and prepared to fulfill your substitute teaching duties under a variety of circumstances. Supplies can be easily carried in a bag, backpack, or attaché case. Below, I list a few essential contents. As you gain more classroom experience and become familiar with your school(s), you will undoubtedly find items that you want to add to your sub pack.

Blank paper or blank substitute teacher report

You will need to inform the regular teacher of what took place in his or her absence, and paper might not be ready at hand. The Things to Do After School list in Chapter 3 contains more information about what to include in your report. You may also use the form letters in Resources C and D at the end of this book.

Pen

A very simple item, but as with paper, pens may have been locked away in the teacher's absence. A report scrawled on a sheet of paper towel with a crayon doesn't look terribly professional.

Chalk and dry-erase markers

Bring these just in case the chalk or markers in the classroom have been locked away, or you can't find them.

Index cards or self-adhesive name badges

Index cards can be folded in half to create nametags that sit on students' desks. Or name badges can be stuck to students' shirts, if you prefer. Naturally, badges are best if your students will be moving around the room rather than sitting at their desks or worktables. Giving students a few minutes to write their names and decorate their cards or badges can give you a peek into their personalities and can also keep them from getting bored while you take attendance.

Whistle

This is a good item to have if you substitute teach physical education classes at the secondary level or supervise the playground at recess time for younger students.

Tissues

These are good to have on hand for a runny nose—yours or someone else's—and there might not be a box in the classroom.

Food

I recommend that you pack a lunch and some snacks for yourself unless you are absolutely certain that there will be food for sale on campus or nearby.

A bottle of water

Teaching can be thirsty work, and you mustn't leave your students unsupervised to go in search of a drink.

Small bag for money, keys, and a driver's license

I have met more than one sub who used a hidden money belt for this purpose. Do not bring any valuables to school that you don't need. (See Chapter 6 for more information about protecting your belongings while at work.)

Age-appropriate story books or books of emergency games and activities

Always follow the lesson plans that have been left for you by the regular teacher. However, it's nice to have some short stories or activities ready in case there is extra time to fill. Also, if your students demonstrate good behavior, you may reward them by filling in extra time by reading a short story aloud or leading them in a game. The titles of activity books are listed in the Suggested Readings section at the end of this book. Please also consult Resource E for a list of Web sites that offer free materials for use by teachers and subs.

WELCOME BACK, KOTTER: TEACHING WHERE YOU WERE ONCE TAUGHT

In case you aren't familiar with the mid-1970s television show *Welcome Back, Kotter*, the story is that of a teacher who returns to his old inner-city Brooklyn high school to teach. He even gets assigned to the same type of remedial class in which he used to be a student, and he works with a group of students that includes a young John Travolta.

If you find that, as a sub, you have the freedom to choose the schools at which you work, and you are subbing in the same area in which you were once a student, this question may arise: Do you want to teach at the schools you used to attend? When I first began to substitute teach, I made a concerted effort to avoid my old schools because I thought that working as a sub on such familiar territory would feel incredibly strange. However, within a few weeks, I was accepting about half of my assignments at my old schools and half at schools with which I was unfamiliar. Why? Because I discovered that both options had their advantages.

I found two key advantages to subbing on familiar territory, especially as a first-year sub. First, I knew many of the teachers and administrators, as well as one principal. Moreover, they remembered me. That familiarity helped me feel comfortable and confident about my work. It also meant that I knew exactly where to go and whom to speak with should any difficulties arise.

Second, I knew the layout of the campuses and locations of most of the classrooms. This knowledge reduced my potential stress levels because I wasn't in any danger of getting lost on the big, sprawling campuses.

By subbing at familiar schools, I found that instead of spending time familiarizing myself with a school and introducing myself to faculty and staff, I could simply go where I needed to go and focus on doing my job well. By accident, I discovered that one of my elementary school classmates was doing much the same thing! She spent most of her time subbing at the school we once attended together and often subbed for one of our former teachers.

On the other hand, exploring different schools in the district was beneficial for me in other ways. First, working at a wide variety of schools enabled me to learn about facets of the public education system with which I had previously been unfamiliar. For example, I had never attended an alternative high school, a school for adults, or a newcomer school, so I enjoyed learning about them through substitute teaching.

Second, working at many different schools enabled me to meet many other subs, regular teachers, and administrators, thus expanding my networking capabilities. (For more information about networking, please see Chapter 4.)

So if you have the opportunity to substitute teach at schools with which you are familiar, give the matter some thought and do what is best for you.

TIPS TO TAKE WITH YOU

- If you have not yet been hired as a substitute teacher, use the Resources section of this book to find out how to qualify in your state.
- Once you have been hired, be sure to arm yourself with key information before reporting for work on your first day.
- When you report for work at a school site, first visit the main office to let the school know that you have arrived and to collect necessary information and materials.
- Be aware of your professional and legal responsibilities as a substitute teacher.
- Remember to prepare yourself for a day of substitute teaching by bringing a bag of useful materials to school.

FOOD FOR THOUGHT

I have listed a lot of materials and information to be collected from or about your school site(s). Once you have collected all that you need from the district office or school(s), you can keep it organized in a folder or a three-ring binder and refer to it easily as needed. In addition to my suggestions in this chapter, what else do you want to know about your schools? What other information and resources do you suggest substitute teachers in your area avail themselves of?

____

____

____

____

____

CHAPTER THREE

General Classroom Procedures

In this chapter, I want to provide you with some example schedules and basic information designed to help you fill a teacher's shoes for a day, or perhaps for several days in a row. There are key steps that you can take before, during, and after class to ensure that your responsibilities are met and your workday progresses as smoothly as possible. Hopefully, after spending some time in your school(s), you will be able to customize my lists to better suit your individual needs and teaching style. Finally, I touch on the subject of lesson planning. The ability to create a basic lesson plan is usually needed more by long-term subs than by short-term ones, but I would rather have that ability and not use it than need it and not have it.

SAMPLE SCHOOL SCHEDULES

School and/or class schedules vary widely across the United States, within states, and even within school districts or between schools. However, there are standards regarding what material students should master at each grade level and how many hours they should spend in class each day and throughout the school year. Although I cannot promise what each day will be like as a substitute teacher, I can provide you with a few sample schedules. I created these after examining class schedules at many different schools in different states and identifying common trends. Of course, exact times and organization of activities will vary in different classrooms, but you can rely on the examples below as rough guidelines of what you can probably expect when subbing.

A Day in Kindergarten

Figure 3.1 is an example of a full day of kindergarten. Some children attend kindergarten for only a half day.

Figure 3.1 Example Kindergarten Schedule

8:50 a.m.	Teachers' daily meeting (some schools provide breakfast for low-income students)
9:20	Class begins; students practice basic skills and prepare for the activities of the day
9:45	Each child chooses from a selection of activities such as art, computers, puzzles, math, looking at books, and so on
11:15	Story and snack time
11:45	Physical Education or a music lesson
12:15 p.m.	A lesson incorporating math, social studies, or science
12:40	Lunch
1:20	Bathroom break
1:45	Recess
2:05	Again, children choose from a selection of activities such as art, computers, puzzles, math, writing, reading, and so on
3:15	Students pack up their belongings
3:25	Students are dismissed

A Day in Elementary School

The schedule in Figure 3.2 is representative of what you might see in first through sixth grades. Subjects will appear in a different order in different classrooms, and some schools offer different subjects and/or activities.

Figure 3.2 Example Elementary School Schedule

8:00 a.m.	Teacher checks attendance
8:10	Reading
8:40	Tuesday: Music lesson Thursday: Students visit the school library
9:15	Science
10:00	Social Studies
10:40	Physical Education
11:10	Snack and bathroom break
11:30	Language Arts
12:45 p.m.	Lunch
1:20	Read aloud/story time
1:35	Math
2:20	Art or Drama
3:05	Students are dismissed

A Day in Secondary School

The example in Figure 3.3 is for a high school math teacher's day, without block scheduling. This scheduling pattern is generally also used in middle schools. Wherever you sub, it is likely that a printed class schedule will be available.

In this case, the regular teacher would probably leave you three different one-hour lesson plans—one for each math level. As the substitute, you should check the schedule to be sure that you are using the right plan at the right time.

Occasionally, schools may implement alternate schedules to accommodate special afternoon events, assemblies, faculty meetings, and other reasons that require students to be dismissed earlier than usual. You can find out if an alternate schedule is being used on the day that you report for work by asking someone in the main office.

Figure 3.3 Example Secondary School Schedule

8:00–8:50 a.m.	1st period	Preparation time (or *prep period*)
8:56–9:46	2nd period	Geometry
9:52–10:42	3rd period	Algebra 2
10:48–11:38	4th period	Geometry
11:44 a.m.–12:20 p.m.	Lunch	*Note: Some junior high and high schools have several different lunch periods.*
12:26–1:16	5th period	Trigonometry
1:22–2:12	6th period	Algebra 2
2:18–3:08	7th period	Supervise Independent Study

THREE IMPORTANT "TO-DO" LISTS

The following lists will help you prepare for the school day, conduct class, and then prepare to leave at the end of the day in an orderly fashion. These lists will probably seem like common sense; however, every item is important, and many get overlooked or forgotten by substitute teachers. A busy school day can be hectic and full of distractions, so use these lists to ensure that you don't overlook anything.

Things to Do Before Class

You can start your day on the right foot by being prepared for the students' arrival. Whenever possible (unless you have been called to work on very short notice), make a point of entering your classroom *before* the students walk, run, or tumble into the room. I recommend giving yourself about 20 minutes to collect your paperwork from the main office, find your classroom, settle in, and deal with any unexpected problems. Some schools require substitutes to arrive a given amount of time before classes begin, but even if yours does not, try to spend enough time alone in your classroom to complete the items in the following list:

1. Read the instructions that have been left for you by the regular teacher.
2. Orient yourself in the classroom by quickly looking around. Locate the teacher's desk and intercom (if available). Are the desks in rows, groups, a circle, or another formation? Groups can sometimes imply that the class is student centered, whereas rows may indicate that the regular teacher has a more teacher-centered style.
3. If they weren't given to you in the main office, locate and read the teacher's instructions for the day.
4. Locate the materials you will require for the day (even if this only includes chalk or a dry-erase marker).
5. Look to see if classroom behavior rules or expectations are posted on a wall.
6. If there is an assignment or information to be written on the blackboard (or dry-erase board), do it now. This step will help prevent you from losing the attention of the students because you won't have to turn your back on them to write.
7. Write your name on the board, particularly if you don't want the students to call you "teacher" all day long.
8. *Optional:* Write a brief outline of the plan for the day on the board. Doing so can attract students' attention and help you engage them in the lesson because they will know what to expect. It can also encourage them to take some responsibility for working through all of the day's tasks in a timely manner. Moreover, it can serve as an easy reference for you to glance at throughout the day.
9. If the class in which you are subbing has a paraprofessional, or teacher's aide, introduce yourself and outline the plan for the day. Find out what the aide's usual role is in the classroom and whether he or she has any helpful information to share.

Things to Do During Class

Once your students are in the classroom (or perhaps before), you will probably become the top news story of the day. Students are sometimes told to expect a substitute, but more often than not it comes as a surprise. You can give yourself the best chance of a smooth, low-stress day by confidently taking charge of the class. What I mean by this is that you need to attract the students' attention, introduce yourself, clearly explain your rules and expectations, and inform them of their responsibilities for the day or the class period. I suggest doing all of this in your best firm but pleasant tone of voice. If this is one of your first substitute teaching assignments and you are nervous, don't let it show (through giggling, hesitation, and so on). Also, don't forget to smile. Smiling can help you to maintain a positive attitude and make your voice sound more pleasing to the ear.

Because you are not the students' usual teacher, class cannot proceed as usual. Rather than pretending that it can, embrace the fact that the day will be a little different. With your positive attitude and confident demeanor, start your class by working your way through the following steps.

1. Get the students' attention and establish quiet so that you can speak to them.
    - Begin class on time. If your school has a bell that announces the beginning of class, address your class as soon as the bell stops ringing. This should be the easiest time to draw all attention to what you have to say.
    - Try out some different first words and choose the opening line that works best for you. One of my favorites is a very loud and upbeat "All right-y then!"

2. Introduce yourself.
    - It's obvious that you are not the teacher who is usually in the room, so briefly let the students know who you are. Begin with your name. You might also tell them something interesting about yourself. They will probably be curious about who you are and how you are going to affect the progression of their day. For more ideas, take a look at Chapter 5.

3. Check and record the attendance.
    - You are responsible for accurately maintaining the record of who is and isn't in class. Call each student by name,

and try to work your way through the list as rapidly as possible, especially if the class is on the large side. If you take too long, students may become bored, and that can lead to disruptions. While you check attendance, it can be a good time to let your students create nametags. Check attendance at the beginning of the day in elementary schools and at the beginning of each class period in secondary schools where new students arrive for each class, unless your school instructs you to do otherwise. As an alternative to reading each name off a list, try asking students to tell you their names. This may help you both hold their attention and avoid mispronouncing names.

4. *Briefly* list your behavioral expectations for the students if you deem it to be necessary.
   - Students are usually accustomed to following a set of rules in the classroom, and these rules may be posted on a wall. If so, hold the students responsible for adhering to these, rather than giving them new rules for the day. However, if you don't see any posted rules . . .
   - Have a few basic behavioral expectations in mind, and briefly tell the students what they are (e.g., no shouting, no leaving the room without permission, no throwing things). If you are in a classroom with student behavior rules posted on a wall, then this step might be unnecessary. In any case, make your expectations simple, achievable, appropriate to the grade level, and clear. Do not discuss disciplinary action or make threats. Students usually can't resist testing a substitute teacher to see how far they can go. Be firm, but fair, and see Chapter 5 for more information about student discipline.

5. Briefly outline the plan for the day/period.

6. Proceed with the lesson plan.

7. Monitor students as they work on an assigned task.
   - While students are engaged in a task either individually or in small groups, walk among them rather than sitting behind the teacher's desk. By moving around the room, you can monitor student progress and provide assistance as necessary. Additionally, your presence will help them remember that there is an authority figure in the room.

8. Reserve the last few minutes of class time for students to clean up the room.
   - If furniture has been rearranged, books or materials have been taken off shelves, or there is writing on the board, have the students put everything back in order. Make sure that all classroom supplies have been returned to their proper locations. No teacher wants to return after an absence to a messy room, and a sub shouldn't have to clean up alone after school.

Things to Do After School

When you dismiss the students and you are, once again, alone in the room at the end of the school day, there are a few things to do before going home. The items on the list below shouldn't take more than a few minutes of your time, but they are an important part of wrapping up your day and handing the metaphorical reins back to the regular teacher.

1. Double-check that the classroom is in the condition in which you found it and that all supplies have been returned to their proper locations.

2. Write a closing note to the teacher.
   - Give a very brief description of the day, and mention any major occurrences or discipline issues.
   - Indicate how much of the lesson plan you taught. If you deviated from the plan, indicate whether you ran out of time, ran out of material, or had some other difficulty. This will inform the teacher of what to begin with on the following day and help him or her prepare for the next sub.
   - If you would like to sub for this teacher again, say so, and leave your name and contact information if permitted.
   - Leave your phone number and invite the teacher to contact you with any questions if permitted.
   - You may write your own brief report for the regular teacher or copy and fill in one of the form letters in Resources C and D at the end of this book.

3. Secure the room.
   - Close and secure any windows that have been opened.
   - Be sure to collect all your belongings and lock the door behind you (if you have been given a key).

4. Visit the main office to return any keys or supplies that were entrusted to you at the beginning of the day and to let the school principal or secretary know that you are leaving. If you left a time card or time sheet at the office, be sure to collect it.

5. Ask if you will be needed the next day.

WORKING TOGETHER: PARAPROFESSIONALS

Teachers in special education, bilingual education, and some other classrooms often have paraprofessionals to assist them. Sometimes called *para-educators* or *teacher's aides*, they have a wealth of experience and information regarding students, classroom procedures, and more. If you find yourself substitute teaching in a classroom in which a paraprofessional is present, introduce yourself and consider the following two points:

- *Questions:* After reading the lesson plan, feel free to ask the paraprofessional any questions that you have regarding classroom rules and routines, the students, specific roles and responsibilities, and so on. You can value the paraprofessional's experience and expertise, and learn from it, without diminishing your own authority.
- *Responsibilities:* The paraprofessional's familiarity with the classroom and the students can help make your day a success. Find out what his or her usual roles and responsibilities are, but remember that the paraprofessional is not the substitute teacher. You are. Let the paraprofessional do his or her job, but don't forget to do yours. You are the teacher, and it is still your responsibility to ensure that the lesson plan for the day is carried out.

LESSON PLANNING IN A NUTSHELL

Successful substitute teachers are always prepared. Subs who drop into a classroom for just one day, or a half day, are usually provided with a lesson plan. Teachers who expect to be absent on a given day (perhaps for a doctor appointment, professional development meeting, or other reason) usually leave behind a plan for the sub to follow. In the event of an unexpected absence (e.g., due to a sudden illness), teachers should have an emergency lesson plan on file somewhere, either in the classroom or in the main office. However, regardless of these precautions, substitutes across the country occasionally find themselves facing a room full of children, teenagers, or adult learners without a plan. Part of the substitute teacher's role is to be prepared for such an eventuality.

I say this with the hindsight of someone who, at one time, was not so prepared. Several years ago, I was called at the last minute to fill in for an alternative high school social science teacher and was told on the telephone that I would find a lesson plan on the teacher's desk, ready for use. Unfortunately, as I explained the assignment to the first class of the morning, the students informed me that they had already completed the entire assignment with the previous day's substitute teacher. They were even able to show me evidence of the fact. To make a long story short, resources in the room were limited and that was the longest 50-minute class period of my life. Obviously, the teacher had not left me a previously used plan on purpose, but everyone makes a mistake now and again, and I should have had a backup plan with me.

So how can you avoid being left to panic without a plan? Bring one of your own to school to use as a backup in case one hasn't been prepared for you. For suggested guidelines to follow when preparing a lesson plan, read on. If you are a short-term sub and are not inclined to design your own emergency backup plans, ready-made lessons for all subjects and grade levels can be found, free of charge, on the Internet by typing the search keywords *lesson plan* and the desired grade level and/or subject area. Online sources of lesson plans are listed in Resource E at the end of this book.

Subs who accept long-term assignments often need to plan their own lessons. This can be a daunting task for someone who has never done it before, but it can be done. The more you prepare, teach, and revise your lessons, the easier the process will become. There are many variations on lesson plans, but most experienced teachers agree on what essential components one should contain. Below you'll find an outline and some advice for creating a lesson plan that you can use whether you are working in a long-term teaching assignment or simply want to create your own emergency backup lessons for your short-term jobs. Knowing the necessary components can also aid you in evaluating, selecting, and adapting ready-made lesson plans that you locate elsewhere. See Suggested Readings and Resource E for sources of free lesson plans.

Lesson Plan Template

I. **Goals:** What overall purpose or goal do you hope to achieve by teaching this lesson?

II. **Objectives:** What exactly will the students learn? What will they practice? What will they do? What will they discuss?

III. **Materials and equipment:** What supplies will you need to teach this lesson? Will you need blank paper? A photocopied handout? A CD player? Twenty pairs of scissors? Do you plan to bring these materials with you or look for them at the school site?

IV. **Procedures:** These can vary widely, but here is a rough set of guidelines that can serve as an example.

   A. You introduce the lesson content and/or conduct a warm-up activity.

   B. You give information and instructions to the class as a whole.

   C. Students work on a task in small groups or in pairs.

   D. The class discusses the information and/or task.

   E. You make your closing comments.

V. **Evaluation:** You will need some means of finding out if the learning objectives that you set out for the students have been met or not. This doesn't have to be a formal test or even a short quiz, particularly if you are with a group of students for only one day or so. Evaluation doesn't even have to be a separate step in your plan. You could simply evaluate the students' understanding of the material by eavesdropping on their group discussions or observing their work. You may also ask the students to informally evaluate their own progress.

VI. **Extra work:** This is sometimes called *homework*, but doesn't need to be done at home. If you are subbing in a classroom for one day, then assigning homework is probably a superfluous step. However, extra work is useful for extending and solidifying your students' new knowledge. Also, having an extra practice activity on hand is important in case some or all of your students finish the other material before the end of class and need something more to do.

Things to Remember When Planning a Lesson

When creating your own lesson plans, please bear in mind the following:

Sequencing

Introduce the topic, perhaps through an anecdote, a series of thought-provoking questions, or just a brief explanation. Then provide your students with some background information with which to work (perhaps written, spoken, pictorial, or all three) before setting them loose to work on a project or task.

Timing

You should always take a guess as to how long each phase of your lesson will take, but monitor the students and be prepared to adjust the timing as needed. Have an extra activity ready in case the lesson proceeds more quickly than you expected. Also, be prepared to skip a step or two and wrap up the lesson if you run out of time.

Individual differences among students

When it comes to learning, one size definitely does not fit all. Remember that students come to class with different learning styles, abilities, and ideas. They also differ from each other in cultural background, physical ability, and social development (Gregory and Chapman 2007). Try to present information both in spoken and written form (either as a handout or on the board), offer hands-on activities when possible, and be sensitive to cultural differences.

Student talk versus teacher talk

Students at any grade level tend to become bored and disinterested if the teacher talks too much (say, for an entire hour). Give them a chance to participate by voicing ideas and opinions. However, don't be afraid to talk enough to thoroughly awaken students' interest in the topic, give information, and explain instructions. When teaching, I usually find that I talk to the whole class about 20% to 30% of the time, although the percentage can vary widely depending on the type of class.

Availability of materials and supplies

If you are not familiar with a particular classroom, don't assume that everything you need is readily available or in working order. Inquire in advance, or bring your own supplies.

Postlesson reflection notes

A lesson can usually be improved upon after you teach it one or more times, but only if you reflect on what went well and what didn't. Simply take a moment after class to jot down your thoughts and any changes you would like to try next time. Bear in mind that students are unique individuals, and a lesson that doesn't work well with one class shouldn't necessarily be discarded; it might simply be better suited to a different group of learners (Brown 2001).

When Does a Sub Need a Lesson Plan?

Basic lesson planning is a very useful skill to have. As a long-term sub, general guidelines regarding subject matter, content, and textbooks may be provided to you by the school, but the minute-by-minute plan for each day will often be left to you. On the other hand, as a short-term sub, you might discover that you need to have a plan of your own ready if

- a teacher doesn't have time to leave one for you,
- you can't find the emergency lesson plan,
- the lesson has already been taught or is otherwise outdated,
- the plan is illegible,
- some other unexpected problem arises.

However, please bear in mind that if a feasible lesson plan is left for you by the regular teacher, it should be followed as closely as possible. Of course, you should use your own judgment regarding timing. If you run out of material and need to fill in some time with your own activity, that's fine. Likewise, if the lesson runs long and you don't have time to cover everything on the plan, that's fine also. However, always be sure to (a) follow a regular teacher's instructions to the best of your ability and (b) leave a note explaining what took place during class.

Many teachers, upon learning that I am writing a book for subs, have asked me to mention that they want more information from their substitutes than "The kids were great!" They want to know what took place during class and exactly what material was covered. Teachers will thank you for taking these two steps and be happy to invite you back to sub for them again. For example, here is a story from my perspective as the regular classroom teacher. While teaching an adult ESL course (not subbing), I needed to miss a day, so I prepared a carefully typed and detailed lesson plan and an attendance form for my substitute to use. The sub completely ignored my instructions and taught his own material to my class, putting my students a day behind the other ESL classes in terms of covering coursework needed for a standardized exam. I was left with nothing but a note saying, in effect, "Everything went well." To make matters even worse, he didn't record the student attendance. I appreciated the fact that my classes were covered in my absence, but I would have appreciated it more if the sub had followed my lesson plan, kept my students on track toward their learning goals, recorded the attendance, and left me a detailed note explaining what had taken place in my absence. As a result, I never requested to have that sub return to my classroom.

TIPS TO TAKE WITH YOU

- Arrive at school at least 20 minutes before classes begin so that you have time to familiarize yourself with the schedule for the day, and take a few other preparatory steps that will help your day progress smoothly.
- Keep checklists handy to ensure that you don't forget to take any small yet important steps before, during, and after class.
- Always follow lesson plans whenever they are provided by the school or regular teacher. However, also have a backup plan ready to use in case one is not provided.

FOOD FOR THOUGHT

I developed my three lists of things to do before, during, and after school by working as a sub and by interviewing other subs and regular classroom teachers. However, every substitute teacher's situation is unique. Based on your own job, what can you add to or remove from each of my three lists to tailor them to your needs?

____

____

____

____

____

Chapter Four

Making the Most of Your Position

Teachers need trustworthy substitutes. Many teachers dread the prospect of leaving a class with an unknown substitute teacher who doesn't keep order in the classroom, teach the day's lessons, or leave behind sufficient information about what took place during the teacher's absence. Many also sympathize with the difficulties (particularly regarding classroom management) that a short-term sub faces. Therefore, responsible and reliable subs are a valuable human resource that is often in high demand. In fact, 86% of school districts report difficulties with finding enough quality substitute teachers (Substitute Teaching Institute, 2007).

With these facts in mind, I present this chapter to help you develop a good reputation with the teachers and administrators in your school or district and maintain good faculty relations. In addition to discussing the art of networking at a school site, I explain the benefits of keeping records of your substitute teaching experiences and offer suggestions for doing so in an organized manner. Finally, I guide you through the simple but important process of reflecting on your past experiences as a student and how they might affect your behavior as a substitute teacher.

BENEFITS OF NETWORKING

When I talk about developing good *faculty relations*, I mean a process that is twofold: first, you become a reliable and competent sub, and then you let teachers and administrators know that you are both trustworthy and available to work. Making an effort to develop and maintain good faculty relations can work to your advantage whether you are subbing for the money, the experience, or both. When teachers know that you are reliable, competent, and available, they may specifically request you to sub for them.

Being requested to return repeatedly to the same classroom can benefit you in multiple ways. First, if there is an unusually low demand for subs in your area, it can result in more work opportunities for you. Also, subbing repeatedly for the same teacher can provide you with a sense of familiarity with the students, the classroom, and the course content that you might not otherwise be able to achieve as a short-term substitute teacher. The students will come to recognize you and know what to expect when you are in charge of the class, thus diminishing the inherent disruptiveness and excitement that the presence of a sub can cause. Moreover, a teacher who appreciates your work will probably inform colleagues that you are a good sub to request, thus further expanding your work opportunities.

Some schools and districts hire full-time substitutes who report for work daily and fill in for teachers as necessary. If you are hired as the full-time sub at one school, where you report for work every day and teach in whatever classroom you are needed on a given day, then networking is also important. You are responsible for filling in for any teacher who is absent, and you can do so as effectively as possible by developing clear communication channels and solid professional relationships with teachers.

MEETING AND GREETING 101

Ironically, the nature of a substitute teacher's role requires you to be present when the regular teacher is not. Although some subs do find themselves involved in faculty meetings or brief morning planning sessions, many do not. Hence, it is possible to substitute teach without actually meeting teachers face-to-face. I strongly recommend making every effort to meet school faculty and staff and to cultivate working relationships with them. Communication between substitute teachers and regular teachers benefits not only you, but also the school systems in which you work. To that end, here are some specific steps that you can take:

1. When you report for work at a school site (on your first visit or shortly thereafter), briefly introduce yourself to the principal and/or vice principal, assuming that he or she is available. Just take a moment to say hello and introduce yourself as a sub. If you are comfortable doing so, invite administrators to visit the class in which you are subbing to see you in action. Even if they are too busy to visit, the invitation can send the message that you are confident in your abilities and proud of your work.
2. Introduce yourself to the person or people in charge of substitute arrangements and/or assignments at the school. This is often a secretary or a receptionist in the main office. A smile and a polite greeting will usually serve you well.
3. When on campus, you will probably be busy teaching your class(es) for the day, and the regular teachers on campus will be busy with their own classes and other responsibilities, but you can introduce yourself in a short note. I suggest leaving a note in each teacher's on-campus mailbox or mail slot, which can usually be found in the main office. Please ask the office staff for permission to leave notes for the teachers. Figure 4.1 shows a copy of the form letter that I used to leave, introducing myself to teachers and offering my services as a substitute teacher.

Incidentally, I would like to mention that I re-entered a substitute teaching pool for a few months to refresh my memory of the experience and to test all of my procedural checklists shortly before sitting down to write this book. I followed each of the three steps listed above at an alternative high school and at a newcomer elementary/junior high school. I deliberately did *not* mention my background in the field of education or that I had worked as a sub in previous years. The district in which I worked

Figure 4.1 Letter of Self-Introduction

DATE

Hello!

I am a new substitute teacher in the ___________ School District. I am studying education as a graduate student, and am subbing as a means of determining what grade level I want to teach in the future (and of paying for school).

I can follow lesson plans and manage student behavior, and would be happy to cover for you the next time you need to be absent from your classroom.

Sincerely,

Cicely A. Rude

PHONE NUMBER

used a computerized system that randomly telephoned substitute teachers; however, the staff members in charge of finding subs at each of those two schools bypassed the system and called me personally to substitute teach classes for the rest of the school year. Unfortunately, after the first few months, I had to decline the offers because I had moved on to teaching my own adult ESL class, but the simple practice of introducing myself at schools in a professional manner proved to be highly effective.

STAYING IN TOUCH

When you have finished subbing for the day, leaving behind a clear and polite note for the teacher is a very important end-of-day step. After all of the students have left, please don't forget to sit down at the teacher's desk one last time and do the following:

1. Provide the teacher with details about what you did with his or her class(es).

2. Mention that you would like to sub for him or her again, if you like.

3. If permitted by the school and/or district, leave your name and phone number, or relevant contact information, at the end of the note so that the teacher can do one or both of the following:
   - Ask you to clarify or discuss any information that you wrote in your report at the end of the day
   - Ask you to sub again in the future

4. Write as neatly as you can, as an illegible note will not serve your purposes, and leave it in a highly visible place. If you have reason to believe that your note could get lost among other papers on the teacher's desk, you might want to leave your note in the teacher's mailbox instead. I used to carry brightly colored paper to school with me for the purpose of writing highly visible notes.

If you want to take your networking strategies a bit further, consider printing some business cards for yourself. Doing so ensures that your information looks professional, is easy to read, and is easy for a teacher or administrator to store for future reference. Figure 4.2 is an example of how such a card could look. Feel free to be as creative as you like with your cards, as long as your information is clear and easy to read.

If you only sub at certain grade levels or in specific subject areas, you could indicate that information on your card. Sheets of blank, printable business cards can usually be found online or in stores that sell office supplies and are available in many colors and patterns.

Staying in Touch With People

If your school or district allows teachers to arrange for their own substitutes, and you receive a phone call from a teacher who wants you to sub on a given date, I recommend taking the following steps to keep information as clear and well organized as possible:

- If a teacher personally asks you to substitute teach a class, reply right away with a clear *yes* or *no* answer. Leave no doubt as to whether you are available to sub for that teacher on the

Figure 4.2 Substitute Teacher Business Card

Stacy B. Supersub

Substitute Teacher
Great Kids Unified School District

Available to teach your class M-F

Contact: (123) 456-7890

day(s) in question. The teacher needs to know if he or she has found a substitute. *Maybe* can be a confusing answer.

- Likewise, if a teacher calls and says that he or she might need a sub on a particular day, but isn't exactly sure, I recommend against offering to keep the date open until he or she is certain of the need. Accepting a potential assignment will prevent you from being able to accept other, more definite assignments on that day (unless you don't mind, of course).
- When accepting direct invitations to substitute teach, you can't be too definite about dates. Look at a calendar and don't be afraid to repeat the day and date several times for extra certainty that everyone is looking at the same calendar page. For example, I once agreed to work on Friday, June 29, and then later noticed that June 29 was a Thursday. I quickly had to contact the teacher and find out if I was supposed to teach his class on Thursday, June 29, or Friday, June 30. After that, I kept a calendar by the phone.

- Speaking of calendars, be sure to make note of your upcoming substitute teaching assignments in one. A simple day planner will suffice, as will an electronic version on your personal computer. Not all substitute teaching assignments take place on the very next day after you accept them; some are handed out days or weeks in advance. So be sure to make note of your future assignments. As an added benefit, if any payroll-related confusion arises, you can refer to your planner to recall which days you worked and at which school.

Staying in Touch With Information

Staying in touch with people is important, but staying in touch with information is equally important. A busy substitute teacher in a large school district can easily work for a different teacher every day for months and meet thousands of students, so I strongly suggest keeping a record of your previous assignments. This is different from your calendar of future assignments and can help you master your job in several ways. Some subs thrive on the excitement of walking into a new and unexpected situation every day. However, others (including me) can become fatigued by the newness and variety when every day feels like the first day of school. If you keep a record of your completed assignments and some brief notes on each, after a short time you will have generated a useful logbook that you can refer to when similar assignments arise (e.g., same school, same teacher), and thus be better prepared for them. Resource B, at the end of this book, is a blank Substitute Teacher's Log that you can use to document your substitute teaching experiences.

I used such a logbook to stay on top of my various assignments and introduce an element of familiarity into my job. Of course, at the beginning of a new school year, I had to rebuild my logbook. Figure 4.3 displays a fictitious example of the type of information that I used to record about the teachers I subbed for and what took place in the classes. When called to fill in for a particular teacher for whom I had subbed previously, I could consult my list and arrive at the school fully prepared and with some foreknowledge of what to expect from my day at work.

Figure 4.3 Example Substitute Teacher's Log

Date	School	Times	Teacher	Grade/ Subject	Notes
4/25/07	Everyone's Elementary	Arrive 7:45 a.m. Start 8:00 a.m. End 2:45 p.m.	DeVecchio, R.	4th	Class has lots of energy. Lesson plan easy to understand, but bring extra material just in case. One hour with music teacher on Thursdays.
4/26/07	Massive Middle School	Arrive 7:30 a.m. Start 7:50 a.m. End 3:07 p.m.	Campbell, G.	7th and 8th grades Periods 2, 3, 7: 7th-grade Math Periods 1, 4: Pre-Algebra Periods 5, 6: 8th-grade Algebra	Lesson plan provided, but students went a little crazy at first sight of a sub. Took five minutes to calm them down, then no problems. Remember to watch the door. Be firm.

APPLYING THE 13,000-HOUR APPRENTICESHIP OF OBSERVATION TO SUBSTITUTE TEACHING

Even though your students may have a difficult time imagining you sitting in a geometry class and passing notes to your friends, every teacher was once a student. Over the years, numerous teacher educators have recognized that the way people are taught during their school careers has a substantial impact on how they, in turn, teach. Not including preschool, we spend about 13 years in primary and secondary schools, followed by another 4 years in college. As a result, everyone who becomes a teacher in the United States has spent thousands of hours watching other teachers, interacting with them, and participating in their work. Lortie (1975) called this phenomenon the *13,000-hour apprenticeship of observation.*

Whether we mean to or not, we cannot help but internalize some of our teachers' behaviors. According to M. Kennedy (1990), "teachers acquire some seemingly indelible imprints from their own experiences as students and these imprints are tremendously difficult to shake" (p. 17). As a result, after completing teacher certification programs, it is not uncommon for new teachers to fall back on behaviors that they observed while in elementary or secondary school:

> By the time we receive our bachelor's degree, we have observed teachers and participated in their work for up to 3,060 days. In contrast, teacher preparation programs usually require (about) 75 days of classroom experience. What could possibly happen during these 75 days to significantly alter the practices learned during the preceding 3,060 days? (p. 4)

The power of our observations to shape our teaching is especially pertinent to new substitute teachers, many of whom receive little or no training before beginning their work. In fact, 90% of the school districts in the United States give fewer than four hours of training to new subs (Substitute Teaching Institute 2007). Substitutes, as well as regular teachers, are generally inclined to repeat classroom behavior that was modeled for them as students. Rather than ignoring this inclination, subs can use it in a productive way. I therefore suggest that you, as a substitute teacher, can benefit from taking the following two steps:

1. Reflect on your past experiences as a student and the classroom behaviors that your teachers modeled.
2. Based on your experiences, consciously decide which of your past teachers' behaviors, attitudes, and teaching styles you would like to emulate and which you would not.

The Learner's Autobiography

One particularly useful way to reflect on your experiences as a student is to create a learner's autobiography (Bailey et al. 1996). Originally intended to help language teachers reflect on their experiences as language learners, the autobiography is easily adapted to suit the needs of other educators, including subs. To create your own learner's autobiography, first put this book down (temporarily) and think about your school days. Are there any teachers in your past that you particularly admired and respected? Are there any teachers that you would rather not become? After taking some time to brainstorm, jot down answers to the following questions:

1. What are some of the learning experiences you have had, and how successful have they been? How do you judge which were successful and which were not?
2. What can you learn about effective and ineffective teaching from reading your answer to Question 1?
3. How might your experiences as a student influence the way you behave as a substitute teacher (Bailey et al. 1996)?

RESPECTING CULTURAL DIVERSITY

Reflecting the cultural diversity of our immigrant nation, school classrooms are very culturally diverse (Wilke 2003). When you walk into a classroom as the substitute teacher and look around at your students, every pair of eyes looking back at you represents unique cultural roots. The demographics of American students are constantly changing (Banks 1994; Nieto 2000), which isn't surprising when we consider that the diversity index in this country is 49% (United States Census Bureau 2000). That statistic means that if two people were randomly selected, there would be a 49% chance that they would differ in ethnicity.

Teachers and substitute teachers interact with diverse young people on a daily basis. According to Schneidewind and Davidson (1998),

> as teachers in a pluralistic society we encounter an exciting challenge every time we enter the classroom. We interact with diverse young people with whom we strive to create a classroom community where all can learn together in an equitable, challenging and happy way. The lessons we teach students about living in this diverse community, as well as the knowledge and skills gained from academic subjects, prepare them for life in our democratic society. (p. 5)

While teachers have the advantage of getting to know their students and developing their classroom culture over the course of the school year, as a substitute, you can also foster equality and respect student diversity. When you walk into a classroom and meet a group of students for the first time, teach them with the following implications of equality in mind:

- Value everyone and treat everyone fairly.
- Respect everyone, regardless of his or her social group.
- Provide everyone with equitable opportunities.

TIPS TO TAKE WITH YOU

- Reliable and trustworthy subs are a valuable human resource. As a result, you can benefit from doing your job well and letting teachers know that you are available to sub for them again in the future.
- With permission from your school and/or district, consider using letters of introduction and homemade business cards, and keeping detailed records.
- Take a few moments to reflect on your experiences as a student and consciously decide which of your former teachers' behaviors you wish to emulate and which you do not. A learner's autobiography is an excellent tool for reflection and conscious decision making.
- As a teacher, model respect for the cultural diversity represented in America's classrooms.

FOOD FOR THOUGHT

Take a few minutes to answer the following questions, and use your answers to prepare your own letter of introduction:

1. How many days per week are you available to work? Which days?

2. At which schools are you both qualified and willing to work?

3. At which grade levels are you both qualified and willing to work?

4. If you plan to sub at the secondary level (junior high and high school), which subjects are you both qualified and willing to teach?

5. Why should a teacher request you to substitute teach? For example, are you experienced? Enthusiastic? Energetic? Responsible?

___

___

___

___

___

Chapter Five

Eight Classroom Management Tips to Make Your Job Easier

Classroom management is a term that gets bandied around quite a bit, but what does it mean? For the purposes of this chapter, I define it as everything a teacher does to direct what happens in a classroom. Ideally, a teacher can use classroom management strategies to ensure that students spend as much time as possible *on task*, or engaged in the learning process.

A substitute teacher's job is to supervise students and keep them generally on track toward the prescribed educational goals until their regular teacher can return. However, subs disrupt the usual class routine with their very presence. After all, part of the usual routine involves the regular teacher being in the room and not being replaced by a stranger. For a substitute, especially in a one-day assignment, classroom management skills are vital for overcoming this initial disturbance and moving the day along smoothly.

Some subs develop their own tricks and strategies for maintaining what they perceive as tight control of the classrooms in which they find themselves. Others simply bring a novel and read quietly while they wait for each class period to end. However, these are extremes. Effective teachers *manage* their classrooms. Students are not robots, so they cannot be directly controlled, but nor should they be left to their own devices. This chapter describes eight strategies that I discovered through research, as well as trial and error, and now pass on to you. If you take them to heart and put them into practice, they can make your job much easier, more relaxing, and more fulfilling than it otherwise might be.

1. ATTITUDE

An evil disposition is infectious.

—Aristotle

You walk into an unfamiliar classroom, and the students who will be with you for the next hour or two, or the next day or two, filter in and sit down. The stage is set. At the great risk of sounding incredibly cliché, it is the beginning of a new day, a *tabula rasa* (clean slate), and you can color it from the outset with your attitude. The students will probably watch you, wondering about the stranger who has entered their classroom. They will probably wonder what immediate effect your presence is going to have on them, and you probably won't get a second chance to make a first impression. As the teacher in charge for the day, you get to set the tone for the class. Hence, a positive attitude can make all the difference.

I learned the importance of a positive attitude the hard way one day when I subbed for an English teacher at a block-schedule high school after sleeping very badly. I crawled out of bed late and had a splitting headache by the time I arrived on campus. I then made the mistake of telling the students in the first period that my day was off to a bad start. The students immediately began to regard me as a grouch and a potential enemy, and the two hours that we spent together were very difficult. Fortunately, thanks to block scheduling, I had a 20-minute break between the first two classes of the day to think about what had gone wrong. When the next group of students arrived, I still had a headache and I was still sleepy, but I greeted them pleasantly with a confident smile and the next two hours went very well.

I realize that substitute teachers are human beings with lives and problems outside of work. However, the first step to keeping your workday problem free is to leave your personal problems at home. I found that my job as a substitute teacher was noticeably easier when I didn't bring thoughts of my nagging headache, looming auto insurance payment, or other personal problems to work with me.

Unfortunately, even if you manage to leave your personal problems at home, as a substitute teacher, you can have difficulty staying positive. A key ingredient to maintaining a positive attitude throughout the day is a healthy sense of humor. Be ready to laugh at situations and at yourself. For example, you are likely to run into at least one or two class clowns for whom a primary source of entertainment is upsetting substitute teachers. Please recognize attempts to get your goat, and ignore them. Remember, the goal of a clown is to cause you to lose your temper. I once had a boy in a junior high school class try to cause a disruption for a solid hour. I alternated between ignoring him and smiling at him, and I paid extra attention to the students who were engaged in the lesson. By the end of the hour, the boy apologized to me for being rude. It turned out that I was the only teacher to not get angry with him as he vied for negative attention. After that, whenever he saw me, he would give me pictures that he had drawn in his art class.

What Would You Do?

Imagine that an elementary school calls you in the morning and asks you to please sub for a third-grade teacher who called in sick at the last minute. They understand that you can't possibly arrive until at least 30 minutes after the beginning of the school day. Another adult will watch over the students until you arrive. You reach the school in the anticipated amount of time, check in at the main office, and then proceed to the classroom with the regular teacher's emergency lesson plan in hand. Unfortunately, the students are irritable, bored, and overly excited by the unusual break from their morning routine. Also, did I forget to mention that you got a speeding ticket on the way to school? Oops. What would you do? Pause for a moment and reflect, then write how you would handle the situation before continuing to read.

____

____

____

____

____

The students need to know that you are confident, competent, and in charge. After all, the speeding ticket and the late timing are hardly their fault. At this point, I would take a deep breath (or several), count to 10 (or higher), and begin the day with a smile.

2. RULES, AUTHORITY, AND LEADERSHIP

You do not lead by hitting people over the head.
That's assault, not leadership.

—Dwight D. Eisenhower

Students and substitutes have an eternal relationship: students see a sub in their room and instantly know that the day is somehow going to be different from other days. I put it to you that you should not expect to be met with automatic respect, love, and obedience simply because you are a teacher and an authority figure. However, neither should you expect to be met with immediate animosity and aggression. I once had lunch with a substitute math teacher who taught me that lesson without actually meaning to. He announced that his favorite strategy for keeping rambunctious students "in line," as he called it, was to instill fear in them from the beginning of the class period. He said that he would select one student, not the noisiest, but the second noisiest, and issue a citation (a slip of paper that the student had to take to the office, indicating his or her offense). That, he claimed, invariably frightened the rest of the class into silence.

I made the mistake of trying his strategy once, and only once, with disastrous results: the students in the class regarded me as an unfair tyrant and went out of their way to be difficult. Their efforts were quite ingenious and I never employed that unfair tactic again. Instead, I learned to establish my authority calmly and with confidence, thus shaping the students' impression of me and earning their respect, instead of their fear and resentment. That was overwhelmingly more effective.

Have you ever heard of self-fulfilling prophecies? Well, here is one that can take place in classrooms: If you regard students as troublemakers and treat them as such, they are more likely to behave like troublemakers. If you treat them like responsible people, on the other hand, they are more likely to behave like responsible people. Of course, this is not an absolute, and good subs always remain on their toes. By showing students that I am not their babysitter, I inadvertently remind them that they are not babies. Your job as a substitute teacher is not to become the best of friends with every student you meet. However, there is no need to invite problems by turning yourself into a *persona non grata*, or an enemy, on purpose.

Classroom management is not unlike business personnel management. What I mean by this is that you can often cultivate comparatively mature behavior in students by awakening their sense of ownership and responsibility, establishing clear channels of communication, and stating your expectations. After introducing yourself to a new group of students, I recommend the following two steps:

1. **State** your expectations and rules clearly. Keep them simple. Do not mention consequences for not following the rules or meeting your expectations, thus indicating that you fully expect them to be followed.

2. **Inform** the class that your job is not necessarily to judge "good" and "bad" behavior. Instead, *all* behavior and class proceedings, whether good, bad, or indifferent, will be reported to the teacher in a note.

Both steps are important, but the second is the keystone. Since you don't hold the ultimate powers that the regular teacher does (e.g., assigning grades, calling parents), you must let students know that the day is not a free-for-all. Subs generally have the disadvantage of not knowing all of the regular teacher's rules, regulations, or procedures, not to mention his or her personality. Students know this and sometimes like to see how much they can get away with. This lack of knowledge can be a substitute teacher's biggest challenge, so here is my best-kept secret remedy: Tell the class that you are just like a video camera and that all the events of the day, good, bad, and indifferent, will be included in the report that you leave for their teacher. If students tell you, "Our teacher lets us do this . . ." you can simply answer, "Then he (or she) won't mind when he (or she) hears about it." This strategy has averted a lot of problems for me by taking some of the responsibility for monitoring acceptable behavior and class proceedings off my shoulders and placing it on the shoulders of the students. As a sub, you are not expected to be a psychic phenomenon, so if students insist that something is normal procedure and are prepared to proceed accordingly (assuming that it is not obviously wrong), just include it in your report.

Interestingly, the regular teacher's manner and classroom management style can affect the attitudes and behavior of his or her students toward a substitute. Consider these three possible scenarios.

1. If the teacher has tapped into the students' motivations and arranged for the students to be responsible for their own learning and behavior, and the class is relatively self-sufficient, then too much "meddling" on your part can actually cause problems.

2. If the teacher is very controlling and the students have come to resent being ruled with an iron fist, so to speak, they are likely to cheer emphatically upon discovering that they have a substitute and regard the day as party time, making it difficult for you to keep them on task.

3. If the teacher has established a systematic routine and strict rules for behavior in class, and the students are used to that routine and assume some ownership of those behavior rules, you might find that they keep themselves to their regular pattern even without the regular teacher present.

In the first and third scenarios, too much interference from you can disturb the class routine and result in difficulties, so I recommend that you interfere only as necessary, adopting a philosophy of *quieta non movere* (leave settled things alone, or let sleeping dogs lie). In the second scenario, it will be necessary for you to establish clear ground rules and inform students that your presence does not mean that the day should be a free-for-all, following the two points mentioned above.

In any case, help students understand that you *are* an authority figure and that you are *not* their enemy. Never show uncontrolled anger, never let the students see you sweat (unless you are teaching a physical education class), and never let them see you cry. When it comes to temporarily managing someone else's classroom, a smile and a sense of humor are worth their weight in gold.

What Would You Do?

Suppose that you find yourself subbing for a high school journalism teacher. At the beginning of their regular class period, the eleventh- and twelfth-grade students on the staff of the school newspaper enter your classroom and begin to work on their respective projects. They seem to be on task, responsible, and committed to their work. Do you interrupt them to give a minilecture about good behavior, emphasizing the importance of not throwing things or speaking out of turn, or would you take another approach? What would you do? Take a moment to write your thoughts below before continuing to read.

____

____

____

____

____

These students seem to be in the process of successfully managing their own behavior and working toward an appropriate and previously established goal. I would simply get their attention to briefly introduce myself and mention that I am available to help as needed.

3. USING A GIMMICK

You gotta have a gimmick.

—Ethel Merman

A *gimmick,* or something interesting that you say or do to get your student's attention, is not a necessity for substitute teachers, but it can be a useful tool. As Gaither (1998) notes, "each individual has gifts and talents that they should utilize to captivate children. Use what you have or what you can do to enhance your relationship with children" (p. 11). Students are not robots. Neither are teachers. Therefore, I encourage you to enhance your rapport with your learners by being yourself. Age-appropriate stories, wisdom, experiences, jokes, and special talents that you have acquired during your journey through life can be valuable assets in the classroom. By bringing a little bit of who you are to school, you may be able to have a positive impact on the many impressionable learners that you meet in the capacity of a substitute teacher.

A gimmick can be something as simple as a brief introduction of yourself, including your least favorite food, the time you accidentally ate a bug, or something interesting that you once did. It can be more elaborate than that if you wish, but the purpose is simply to grab the students' attention and get the class started on a positive note.

When coming up with a gimmick, you have to be true to yourself. For example, a fellow graduate student of mine used to substitute teach once in while, and each time he would bring his guitar with him. He would begin and end each class by performing humorous songs. He was adored by students at the local schools, who would work diligently during class so as to give him time to play at the end of class.

If you work in high schools, and if the students are receptive to it, the beginning of class can be a good opportunity to tell students about the benefits of attending college. Some high school students don't have any family members with college educations, and you can serve as an example for them. You might collect brochures and financial aid information from nearby universities and community colleges and make these resources available to the students in classes that you visit as a substitute.

As for me, I enjoy traveling and living in different countries. As a result, I have several introductory speeches that I have used in classrooms, each less than two minutes in length, about things that I have experienced in various exotic locations. In one of these speeches, I ask for a show of hands of which students would like to visit other countries some day. I then mention that I spent a year as a college exchange student in Australia, where I went scuba diving at the Great Barrier Reef and came face-to-face with a giant barracuda. At other times, I talk about a dinner party I attended as an English teacher in Japan. During dinner, the entrée of live tiger prawns began to leap off the tables and escape toward the door.

I don't mean to imply that you need to be a great musician or have been chased across Mongolia by wild yaks in order to be a successful substitute teacher. Just take a minute or two at the beginning of class to tell your students a little something about yourself, share something interesting or amusing, and get their attention. Let them know that you are a fellow human being, as opposed to a nameless, faceless substitute.

What Would You Do?

Use the space below to list the grade levels, subject, schools, and programs that are available to you as a substitute teacher. Given your background, special talents, and interests, what gimmick(s) might you use for each?

___

___

___

___

___

4. GETTING TO KNOW THE STUDENTS

I never met a man I didn't like.

—Will Rogers

As a substitute teacher, you are faced with unique challenges. You probably don't have the luxury of gradually familiarizing yourself with students over the course of an entire semester or school year. In fact, you might walk into a new classroom and meet a new group of students every day of the week (and in some cases, every hour of the school day). Moreover, those students are accustomed to being in a room with their own teacher, who probably doesn't look like you and who does things differently than you do. In most cases, you won't even have met the regular teacher in person. What do you do?

There is a limit to how much you can learn about a room full of students in the space of one school day or one class period. However, you can learn some things about them and take action accordingly. I suggest that you observe the students and try to make educated guesses in response to the following questions:

- What are these students interested in? (Money is often a universally good guess.)
- What is the approximate behavioral maturity level of this class? (You can use their behavior and grade level to begin to understand this one.)
- What are the disciplinary needs of these students?

If you find an answer to the first question, you can grab and hold the students' attention and keep them tuned in to the lesson or task at hand. I was once faced with a rather dry remedial math lesson and a room full of high school freshmen who did not want to be in a classroom at all. After they asked me how much I was paid, followed by a few more money-related questions, it occurred to me that they might be interested in talking about money. I turned all of the math problems that I was supposed to demonstrate on the board into money-related word problems and dollar amounts.

I had their attention, and they stayed on task for the rest of our time together. Better yet, I think they actually learned some math.

If you can find answers to the second and third questions, you will have found the keys to managing the class. It is important to manage students appropriately, bearing in mind their individual differences and needs. Acting too strict and rigid with more mature students is unnecessary and will make them feel stifled and resentful of you; they might even rebel and act out in ways that are uncharacteristic of them. Not being strict enough with students who need clear guidelines can lead them to behave inappropriately. Students are individuals with different needs, and some need more rules, guidelines, and discipline than others. Some need clearly defined rules and boundaries, whereas others can govern themselves and hence require fewer guidelines. You will have to make a guess as to the needs of the students in the room because, as I said before, if you are too strict with students who are mature enough to self-govern, they will resent your presence and possibly act out. Likewise, if you offer ambiguous guidelines to students who need to have the rules and boundaries clearly delineated, they might feel lost and act out.

Either mistake results in more work for you, so judge as wisely as you can. Figure 5.1 illustrates the three questions and how seeking answers to them can help you rapidly guess the needs of your students.

If you find that answering the three questions while simultaneously teaching is a difficult task, don't worry. A little experience can give you insight and make it much easier than you might think. Also, there are probably some clues that you can use. For example, some information about the students, such as their grade level, will always be available to you even before a class begins. In addition, you may receive a note regarding students' disciplinary needs from their regular teacher. If it is a high school class, the academic level and course title will appear on the attendance sheet. I recommend using all of this information, combined with your observations of their initial behavior (e.g., Do you have to remind them to be quiet while you are speaking? Do you have to tell them to sit down at their desks when the bell rings?) to quickly make an educated guess regarding the degree of strictness that is appropriate for the class. The more accurately you guess, the more smoothly your class can proceed.

Figure 5.1 Three Questions and How They Can Help

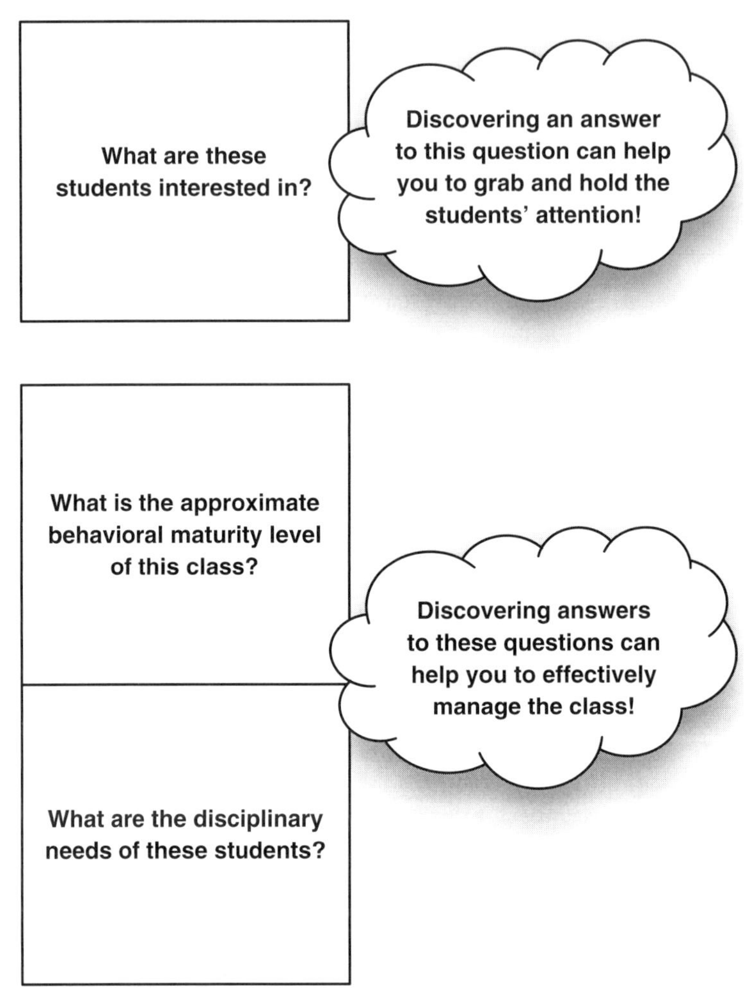

What Would You Do?

You walk into a classroom in which you are to spend the day subbing for a middle school teacher. The students will arrive in about 20 minutes. You look around and notice that the desks are all in rows facing the front of the room. You read the teacher's lesson plan for the day and notice that there is no mention of group work. I would take that as a sign that these students do most of their work individually and might be accustomed to a teacher-centered classroom, possibly with fairly strict rules regarding noise levels. What other clues might you look for before and after the first students arrive? Write your ideas below.

____

____

____

____

____

5. DEALING WITH DISRUPTIONS

What you cannot enforce, do not command!

—Sophocles

Disruptions are bound to occur in even the most carefully managed classrooms, but how you address them is up to you. Therefore, please consider the following pieces of advice:

- Never threaten to take action that you are not fully prepared to follow up on.
- Since threats/statements must be followed up on in a timely fashion, don't make them unnecessarily.
- Don't turn small problems into big ones. It just makes your job unnecessarily stressful and less enjoyable. It also takes away from valuable learning time.

No matter how frustrated you may be, don't make unnecessary or empty threats, lest you find that you have to follow up on them. Unfulfilled threats and promises of action immediately negate anything you may say from that point on. Essentially, you risk sending students the message that you don't mean anything you say and that you may be safely ignored. Students of any age are not robots. Their motivations and behavior at any given time are complex and variable. Even the most well-behaved students are bound to do things that are a bit disruptive or off-task now and again.

Would you believe that teachers sometimes exacerbate or add to discipline problems? Well, it's true! No, I don't mean that teachers are troublemakers who run around trying to cause problems. However, teachers and substitute teachers sometimes respond to small disruptions in ways that turn them into much bigger problems.

Before walking into a classroom, all substitutes should take a moment to consider the behavioral limitations and boundaries that they wish to maintain. For example, how much noise is too much? Bear in mind that some student behaviors, such as physical violence or verbal abuse, are unacceptable under any circumstances. However, most student disruptions are simply due to minor behavioral problems, such as inattentiveness, talking, or peeking out of the window to see friends pass by. When faced with such behavior, I suggest that you ask yourself the following questions:

- Is this behavior unlikely to end of its own accord?
- Is this behavior preventing the offender from learning something?
- Is this behavior distracting other students?

If the answer to these questions is a resounding *yes*, then think about how you can change the behavior while disrupting the class yourself as little as possible. The following is a series of steps that you might take; they have worked for me as well as for other teachers and substitutes:

1. Make eye contact with the offending student. You might include a smile. This nonverbal communication will let the student know that you are not oblivious to his or her behavior and the student may self-correct. If the student does not self-correct, do not assume that he or she is being purposefully disruptive. He or she might be unaware of the problem.

2. If Step 1 doesn't work, stand near the student. Chances are that he or she knows how to behave appropriately in class and will alter the behavior.
3. Approach the student and briefly explain the problem. Tell him or her to alter the behavior.
4. Distract disruptive students by jumping into their conversations and asking relevant questions.
5. If you discover that a student is being intentionally disruptive, elicit his or her help. At the lower grade levels, you might appoint the student to be your assistant for the day, giving him or her both a distraction and a purpose. Keep the student busy by asking him or her to help you pass out papers and perform other tasks.

If you need the attention of a room full of students, or you are talking and the general noise level has become too loud, try this: stop talking and raise a hand in the air. One by one, the students will probably notice. Teach them to stop talking and raise their hands when they see what is happening. A teacher can very quickly get everyone's attention this way. When the room is quiet, begin speaking or resume what you were saying (Warner and Bryan 2006). This method of turning silencing a room into a game is often used at the elementary school level, but I have seen it used successfully at all levels of education, including college, so give it a try.

What Would You Do?

Imagine that you are spending a day as the substitute teacher in a fifth-grade class. While you are trying to give instructions for a task assigned by the absent teacher, two girls keep talking with each other. Not only are they not listening, but they are also distracting the students around them. Do you

(A) stop giving your instructions to ask the girls for their names and to publicly lecture them about the importance of listening respectfully in class

or

(B) walk to where the two chatty girls are sitting and calmly stand between them while continuing to give the instructions?

or

(C) Take a different approach of your own? If so, please explain.

Write your choice or original solution and your reasons below. Then read on for my solution.

____

____

____

____

____

Solution A tends to embarrass some students unnecessarily, prompting them to act out even more, and other children will simply tune out. Worst of all, it takes away from productive class time. You might have a different solution, but my favorite is B. Disruptions such as this one can often be rectified without the teacher saying a word. More often than not, your very proximity will remind students that they are in a classroom and to stay on task.

When substitute teaching (as well as when teaching in your own classroom), it is in your best interests to determine which behaviors are disruptive and which you can afford to ignore. Don't turn small disruptions into bigger ones. Don't make mountains out of molehills. Do choose your battles wisely and exercise flexibility.

6. FLEXIBILITY

The bend in the road is not the end of the road
unless you refuse to take the turn.

—Anonymous

Plans sometimes go wrong. Otherwise cooperative students sometimes act out. Lessons sometimes take more or less time than planned. What do you do? You must judge each situation and handle it to the best of your ability.

A substitute who is able to adjust to different situations and act accordingly is not wishy-washy, but flexible. The ability to be flexible is not a sign of weakness. Instead, it shows that you are comfortable enough in your authority as a substitute teacher to judge situations for yourself, and students, faculty, and staff will generally appreciate that. When subbing, be ready to bend lest you break, but know when to stop.

I have two examples with which to illustrate what I mean in practical terms. For the first, I need to take you back to when I was an impressionable child of 12 or 13. I remember many of my subs, and one in particular who took charge of my seventh grade science class for one day. She was instructed by the regular teacher to show the class a film about railroad safety. It was a shocking and sad video designed to teach us not to play near or on railroad tracks. I remember being very moved by the film, and I occasionally expressed my surprise to the kid sitting next to me with a look or a whispered "wow." We exchanged a few horrified looks during the show, but we were quiet; we were very engrossed in what we were watching. The substitute teacher had been monitoring the class from the back of the room. When the video ended, she launched into a speech about how a student (who had been reading a small comic book on his lap) was a perfect example of how a student should behave respectfully and quietly during an in-class movie. She then moved on to using me as an example of poor behavior, because I had obviously not been paying attention, in her opinion.

I realized at the time that the woman had such a rigid view of good behavior that she completely failed to realize what was happening in her classroom. Instead of feeling calm at the end of the hour, she was furious about a problem that didn't exist. If you, as a sub, are unreasonably inflexible in your expectations and perceptions, it is likely that your students will know, and you will miss out on opportunities to help them grow as learners. You may also see problems that aren't actually there.

My second tale of inflexibility comes from a long-term substitute in a third-grade class. We met one day while subbing at the same school. He was angry about his students' behavior at the end of school on a Friday. As he vented, I learned that the lessons for the day had been completed with about 10 minutes to spare before the final dismissal time. With nothing left on the agenda, the sub asked the class to sit quietly until the final bell sounded. Unfortunately, the children found that to be impossible and looked for ways to pass the time. Listening quietly, I thought to myself that it would be easier to teach ballroom dancing to housecats than to make 36 tired, antsy third-graders silently sit still with nothing to do for the last 10 minutes before their weekend began. He could have saved the students some anguish and saved himself a lot of stress by filling that extra time with a short story, a short class discussion (e.g., "What are you going to do this weekend?"), or a short game. Please check the Suggested Reading section of this book for titles that contain short classroom games and time fillers, as well as Resource E for many free online sources of lessons, activities, and games for all ages, grades, developmental levels, and subject areas.

What Would You Do?

Here are a few more situations requiring flexibility on the part of a substitute teacher. Over the years, these true stories have been reported to me by teachers, substitute teachers, and students. There are no right or wrong answers to these questions, so just take a moment to think about how you might respond in each situation, given your job and personal teaching style. Try to add more details to the scenarios, based on your own experience.

1. You have been instructed to show a film in a tenth-grade English class. One student appears to doze off while sitting upright at his desk but remains quiet, not disrupting any other students. Do you take action or not? If so, what do you do?

____

____

____

2. The regular teacher for a fifth-grade bilingual education class indicates in a note that students can only go to the restroom while carrying the official bathroom pass. Unfortunately, you can't find the official bathroom pass, and a student needs it rather urgently. What do you do?

3. The regular teacher leaves a worksheet and instructions for you to make photocopies for her eighth-grade students. Unfortunately, the school's copy machine is broken. What do you do?

4. You are subbing in an Advanced Placement science class. The students are college-bound juniors and seniors who are behaving in a responsible manner. They are working on projects assigned to them by their regular teacher. They began working even before you checked their attendance. There is a low level of talk throughout the room. Most of it is task oriented, but some isn't. Is this a problem? What do you do?

____

____

____

____

____

7. DEVELOPING MUTUAL RESPECT

When you know me, rebuke me; not till then.

—Sophocles

If you treat students with respect, you give them the opportunity to respect you in return. Granted, sometimes a student has so much bottled-up anger or such poor interpersonal skills that this doesn't work. However, more often than not, students respond favorably and appreciate the respect that is shown to them.

I have always spoken to students as if they were my colleagues, regardless of their age or grade level, bearing in mind that children's brains are still developing. In return, they usually exercise some self-discipline and demonstrate as much behavioral maturity as they can. I behave as if I am there to help and to advise them. Serving as a colleague as well as an authority figure and role model for a room full of students can be difficult, but it is often well worth the effort.

I suggest that you begin by introducing yourself to the class, whether or not you have a gimmick. If you have some special expertise or interest that you would be happy to chat about, let the students know. Another useful strategy can be practiced while taking attendance. Listing every name on the roll sheet and waiting for each student in the room to indicate his or her presence can be a tedious process. The students tend to get bored while you struggle with the names of their classmates, which can lead to disruptive behavior. You can eliminate the boredom factor and let the students know that you are interested in who they are by asking them to say a little something about themselves when you call their names. The following are some questions that you could have students answer when you reach their names on the roll sheet:

- What is your favorite food?
- If you could visit any place in the world, regardless of cost, where would you go?
- If you could choose anything, what would be your dream job?
- Tell me one interesting thing about yourself.

Asking students to tell you a little something about themselves not only shows them that you are interested in them, but also can provide you with a wide variety of answers. Please remember that your students could be a very diverse group. John F. Kennedy (1964) once described the United States as a nation of immigrants, and so it is. You can easily find plenty of gender, ethnic, linguistic, sociocultural, and socioeconomic diversity in one classroom. Some students may have college-educated parents, and some may not. Some may come from wealthy families, and others may receive food stamps and other government aid. Some may be new immigrants who speak English as their second (or third, or fourth) language. If you avoid making generalizations or assumptions about students, you can avoid causing them to feel misunderstood or alienated, and in turn reduce some of the disruptive behavior that can be born of those feelings.

Students of all ages have told me that when I make an effort to find out a little about them, even if we are only together for an hour or so, they feel valued. High school students have let me know that they appreciate it when I offer information about colleges but don't look down on them if they are not interested in attending college. Treating all students respectfully is not a magical guarantee that they will respect you in return. However, it has been known to work.

What Would You Do?

What might you ask kindergarten or primary grade students to tell you about themselves? How about elementary, middle, or high school students? Write your ideas below, try them out in class when possible, and then return to this page to write down the results.

____

____

____

____

____

8. PREVENTING PROBLEMS

It's better to feed one cat than many mice.

—Norwegian Proverb

Most experienced drivers learn to spot potential accidents before they happen. For example, they see a pedestrian standing on the curb and anticipate that he or she might step into the street without looking. They pass a person riding a bicycle and move over a few feet, giving him or her room to possibly swerve or fall over. They pause momentarily before proceeding through an intersection after the light turns green, knowing that someone might run the red light. Of course, pedestrians often look before crossing a street, cyclists don't often swerve or fall over into the path of passing cars, and not everyone runs red lights. However, recognizing when and where accidents *might* happen and subsequently taking precautions can prevent those accidents. In much the same way, successful substitute teachers learn how to recognize when and where classroom disruptions *might* crop up, and they take preventative action. Sometimes the best defense is a good offense.

You don't need to sub for several years, or even for several months, to begin to spot potential sources of problems, such as the following examples, and to eliminate them.

Some teachers keep a radio or a CD player in the room to play background music during class. With a substitute teacher present, the students might want to use the machine to play music of their own choosing, which is not likely to be music that is conducive to studying. Moreover, the students might disagree on what music to play, which could lead to arguments. If I walk into another teacher's classroom to fill in as a sub (before the students arrive, of course) and I see a CD player or a radio, I do one of two things: I hide it in a drawer, or I make a point of telling the class that their teacher has left clear instructions that we are to listen to classical music (even if that isn't true). The former usually does a better job of preventing problems.

It's up to you, the substitute teacher, to decide whether you want to prop the classroom door open. Leaving the door open can invite fresh air in, but it can also invite passing students to poke their heads in and speak to their friends. It can also occasionally invite a student to try to sneak out without asking for permission. When visiting a school as a substitute, particularly if some students' desks are close to the door, I used to keep the windows open and the door closed. Of course, there are some reasons to leave the door open (please see Chapter 6).

My final example concerns those fascinating dry-erase markers and little pieces of chalk. I have taught in the United States and in Japan, including all levels from the first grade to adult school, and I have never worked in a classroom that did not have a chalkboard or a whiteboard on the wall. The blackboard/chalkboard/whiteboard is the quintessential classroom furnishing. Some rooms even have two or three boards. With a substitute in the room and markers or chalk readily available, students can sometimes feel artistically inspired. It's perfectly understandable, really. Teachers can write on the board whenever they want to, but most students can't do so without permission. When I sub in high school or lower grade levels, walk into a room, and see extra dry-erase markers or pieces of chalk in the shelf beneath the board, I do one of two things. Usually I collect all but one before the students arrive and hide them in the teacher's desk until the end of the day, and I keep the remaining one in my pocket when I'm not using it myself. On rare occasions in the past, however, particularly if the students asked to draw on the board, I would tell them that if the class period (for secondary school) or day (for primary school) went smoothly, they could use the last five minutes to draw, but no one would leave the room until the board had been completely erased.

All classes are different, and the items that can lead to difficulties in some classes might be completely ignored in others. At the same time, patterns do develop. To save yourself some potential hassle, all you have to do is remember the little problems that crop up in your classes and discreetly prevent them the next time around.

What Would You Do?

Imagine that you have just walked into a first-grade classroom that is full of supplies and materials. There are six colored markers beneath a dry-erase board, a portable radio/CD player, a big box of crayons, a big box of scissors, a bookcase full of books, and some little pots of paste all in full view and easy reach. Assuming that they are not needed for the day's lessons, which of these things would you hide before the students arrive? Based on my experiences as a sub, I would remove everything except the books. Years ago, when I was a student in the first grade, a little boy stuck paste in my ear. Remembering that incident, I would definitely make the paste temporarily disappear. Based on your own experiences as a young student, and remembering what you longed to play with during lessons, what other potentially problematic items would you look for?

____

____

____

____

____

TIPS TO TAKE WITH YOU

- Be conscious of the attitude you project in class.
- Consider how to best enforce rules and use your authority.
- Consider using an attention-getting gimmick or simply using your talents and personality when subbing.
- Get to know a little about the students in a short period of time.
- Deal with disruptive behavior as effectively as possible.
- Exercise flexibility.
- Try to develop a degree of mutual respect with the students.
- Practice recognizing and preventing potential problems.

FOOD FOR THOUGHT

I developed these strategies while working as a substitute teacher. Now that you have read my eight favorite classroom management tips for substitute teachers, it's time to adapt them to your situation. Can you add some of your own pieces of advice to the list?

____

____

____

____

____

Chapter Six

Staying Safe

This final chapter is a short but important one. I want you to always remember that substitute teaching can be a very positive experience, regardless of your reasons for doing it. However, a wise sub always hopes for the best while preparing for the worst-case scenario. Therefore, this final chapter is intended to offer some advice on how you can protect yourself, your students, your belongings, and school property while you are substitute teaching.

UNFORTUNATELY IT CAN HAPPEN . . .

Sadly, I once met a substitute teacher whose car had been vandalized in a high school parking lot. I met her in a teachers' lounge less than a week after the incident. She was trying to relieve her anger and frustration by sharing her story with sympathetic listeners, so she eagerly told me her tale of woe. She said that she had spent a day subbing in a high school classroom where she had struggled to uphold the school's behavioral standards and had several arguments with belligerent students. After this particularly difficult day, she had returned to the faculty parking lot to find that the paint on her car had been deliberately scratched. She was angry and hurt, her car was not insured against vandalism, and she didn't know if the school district would contribute to the cost of repairs. It was a traumatic experience, but she wanted to continue substitute teaching, although perhaps not at that same high school. Fortunately, the school district was very large, and she had many other schools from which to choose.

Please bear in mind that stories like the one above do not describe a typical day for all substitute teachers. However, taking a few simple precautions can help prevent you from becoming a victim of any unpleasantness at work. Below are some preventative measures that you can take to keep everyone and everything as safe as possible while you are on a school campus in the capacity of a sub.

PROTECT YOURSELF

First, teachers are occasionally accused of improper behavior. Such accusations are sometimes accurate, and sometimes they are not. To reduce your risk of becoming the victim of any untrue accusations or misunderstandings, be aware of your surroundings and keep yourself and your actions as visible as possible at all times. If you find yourself subbing in a classroom with no windows, you might consider leaving the door open to protect yourself against being wrongly accused of improper behavior behind closed doors. However, bear in mind that an open door can sometimes invite distractions and thus jeopardize your control of the class, depending on the students' maturity level. Maintaining anecdotal records, or a journal of what takes place during your workday, can be a useful preventative strategy. If something takes place in your classroom or you take some action that you feel may be questioned, write down the date, time, place, people involved, what action you took, and your reasons for doing so.

Second, familiarize yourself with your school's disciplinary support systems and procedures when you arrive on campus. These may include an intercom or a walkie-talkie (if available), the location of campus security, and/or the standard procedure for sending unruly students out of your classroom (e.g., to the office) if necessary. While subbing, only on rare occasions did I encounter students who did not respond to any of the classroom management methods that I presented in previous chapters, particularly in Chapter 5. Most discipline problems can be diffused, but in the event that you do need help or you feel threatened by an angry student, I recommend finding out what to do at a particular school site before you need to do it.

Third, never argue with a student. Students of all ages sometimes become angry and say things that can be hurtful. However, someone always needs to be the adult, and that someone is you.

I have occasionally seen teachers, both new and very experienced, lose their tempers and argue with students, and it is never a productive use of class time. Instead of arguing about an issue, simply state that the matter in question is not open to debate, and leave it at that.

PROTECT THE STUDENTS

As the teacher and authority figure for the day, you are responsible for exercising due care and caution to ensure the safety of your students. The following are some steps that you can take to protect them from each other, themselves, and dangers such as accidents, fires, and other emergency situations.

First, *never* leave students without adult supervision. If you have a personal emergency and need to leave your classroom even for a short time, contact the school's main office or otherwise find another authorized adult to fill in for you. If you need help, send a student to the office with a message or use the intercom system (if available). Students should not be left alone, even for a short period of time. You need to be present to monitor the safety of students who are in your charge. Moreover, students are not allowed to leave school property during the school day without express permission from the main office. If you work for a district that has a school for adults, and you have opportunities to substitute teach classes in which all students are over the age of 18, these rules are less relevant. Even in those situations, however, I recommend staying in the room with the students at all times.

Second, if a student in your charge is injured, respond quickly and obtain help. Never give students any kind of medication, even over-the-counter painkillers. If a student requires medication, send him or her to the main office or school nurse. Refer all injured students to the office. You may need to fill out an accident report form if one of your students is injured. If this is the case at your school, leave a copy of the report for the regular teacher. If you assist an injured student, avoid making contact with any body fluids, such as blood. In case you have to assist a bleeding student, bring a pair of disposable latex gloves to school and a plastic bag in which to dispose of them after use (*Substitute Teacher Handbook K–12* 2004).

Third, do not allow students to hurt each other. Although some behavioral issues can dissipate on their own or with minimal intervention, physical abuse and verbal abuse are always unacceptable and require your intervention. Before you begin subbing at a school for the first time, ask an administrator about the school's Safe Schools Policy and standard procedures for severe disciplinary problems (e.g., fighting), and be prepared to follow them if necessary. Know what steps to take, who to contact if you require assistance, and how to contact him or her.

Fourth, learn the emergency procedures that have been established for the school and your classroom. These will vary by school and by classroom, so find out what they are each time you sub in a new place. For example, each class on campus probably has a particular location to which you must escort students in case of a fire drill, a real fire, or another emergency. You might substitute teach for years and never find yourself in an emergency situation. However, in case of an emergency, families are relying on you to keep their young loved ones safe. Sometimes the fire alarm means that a fire drill is underway, but occasionally it could signal a real fire. Walk your students to safety, and don't panic. Know how many students are in your charge, and carry your attendance list with you, so that you can rapidly confirm that all of your students are present and accounted for or identify any who are missing.

Fifth, report any signs of child abuse. Report suspected child abuse of any kind to the school principal or to a peace officer immediately.

PROTECT YOUR STUFF

A classroom can be a very busy and bustling environment, and personal items can sometimes disappear mysteriously between classes, when students return from recess, or even during a class. Large amounts of cash, credit cards, and other valuable items that you don't need at work are best left at home or locked in the trunk of your car; you may not have access to a safe place in which to store them during the school day. In addition to your substitute teaching supplies (see Chapter 2), I suggest bringing only the following:

- identification
- car keys

- a small amount of money to buy lunch, if necessary
- any other needed items of little or no value

Never leave the personal belongings that you bring into class unprotected or unattended. One theft can cause a lot of headache that could have been prevented.

Also take steps to protect your car if you drive to work. I recommend making sure that your car is insured against vandalism and accidents in parking lots and knowing the exact amount of your deductible and any other applicable expenses. Some school districts cover automobile vandalism on school property for full-time teachers, but many substitute teachers do not qualify for such benefits. Check with your school, district, or other hiring agency about coverage for automobile vandalism and the frequency of such incidents, because forewarned is indeed forearmed.

PROTECT SCHOOL PROPERTY

While you are in charge for the day(s) of a substitute teaching assignment, the school and regular teacher are relying on you to ensure the safety of all equipment, supplies, and furniture in your classroom. The following are a couple easy things that you can do to drastically reduce the chances of anything being damaged or stolen.

First, when you walk into your classroom in the morning, count the books and materials (e.g., calculators) in the room before students arrive and again just before they leave. I urge you to conduct the second count as discreetly as possible and then call attention to the fact only if something appears to be missing. After all, there is no need to raise the issue of theft with students who otherwise wouldn't think of trying to "borrow" something.

Second, protect the teacher's classroom when you leave at the end of the day. Classrooms are sometimes used for afterschool activities, tutoring, parent-teacher conferences, club meetings, and so on. However, unless you have been instructed to do otherwise, double-check that all classroom doors and windows are secure before you leave. Lock the door if the school has provided you with a key. Always inform the main office before you leave the school so the staff knows that your job is complete and that you are no longer in the classroom. These are very simple but important precautions that you can take to ensure that everything is as safe as it can be when you head home at the end of the day.

TIPS TO TAKE WITH YOU

- Protect yourself from physical danger and accusations of inappropriate behavior.
- Protect the students in your care. Keep them safe from harm, and never leave them unsupervised.
- Protect your personal property. Don't bring anything to school that you don't need.
- Help protect school property. Take steps to prevent materials, supplies, furniture, and other items from being damaged or stolen.

FOOD FOR THOUGHT

Now that you have read my suggestions for keeping yourself, your students, your own belongings, and the school's property safe, it's time to add a few steps of your own. Think back to when you were a student in school at the grade level(s) in which you plan to sub. Can you think of some more precautionary measures to take now that you are in the substitute teacher's shoes? What precautionary measures can you adopt to suit your unique substitute teaching situation?

____

____

____

____

____

A FINAL WORD

Substitute teaching can be a challenging profession, but not an impossible one. With some forethought and preparation, you can succeed as a substitute teacher. There are as many definitions of *success* as there are people in the world, so I suggest that you begin by deciding what the word means to you. Armed with your personal understanding of what it means to succeed, remember each of the following:

1. Learn about the varieties of schools, programs, schedules, and pay scales that are available to subs in your area.
2. Know your duties and responsibilities.
3. Prepare to uphold classroom procedures, use class time productively, and continue students' learning in the absence of their regular teacher.
4. Make the most of your position by meeting colleagues, keeping records on your assignments, and striving to be the best substitute teacher you can be.
5. Develop your classroom management skills.
6. Protect yourself, the students in your charge, your belongings, and school property.

All teachers and substitutes make mistakes now and again, but the successful ones learn from those mistakes and hone their skills because the best teachers are also good learners. As the editors of Don't Sweat Press (2003) put it, "every day offers new opportunities for you to correct past mistakes, acquire new skills, build better relationships, and try out new ideas" (p. 207). I am confident that you can succeed as a substitute teacher and enjoy the satisfaction of a job well done.

On behalf of educators everywhere, I want to thank you for taking on the role of the substitute teacher. Whether this is a permanent or temporary job for you, the work you do is important and much appreciated. I wish you the best of luck!

Resource A: State-by-State Information

The following is contact information for the U.S. Department of Education and the agency responsible for public education in each state. Some agencies have multiple addresses, telephone numbers, or Web addresses. Each agency's main Web site is listed, and many offer job postings and other employment information. If you are not already a substitute teacher, contact your state authority on teacher licensing to find out either what steps you should take to become one or whom to contact.

I have included a brief overview of information regarding substitute teachers in each state, much of which was collected by the Substitute Teaching Institute (2006) and the National Education Association (2002). Find your state in this alphabetical list to learn a bit of background information. Information about pay rates is not included because of variations and frequent changes. Please bear in mind that all the information in this list is intended only to serve as a starting point and that changes in demand for and qualifications of substitute teachers occur frequently. Check with your state education office or local school district main office for changes and details.

U.S. Department of Education Home Page: http://www.ed.gov

Alabama

Alabama Department of Education
Gordon Persons Office Building
50 North Ripley Street
P.O. Box 302101
Montgomery, AL 36104-3833
(334) 242-9700
http://www.alsde.edu/html/home.asp

Substitute teachers must obtain a Substitute Teacher License, which is valid for five years. After five years, the sub must reapply for a new license. The minimum requirement is a high school diploma or the equivalent thereof. School districts may also request fingerprints and a background check.

Alaska

Alaska Department of Education & Early Development
801 West 10th Street, Suite 200
Juneau, AK 99801-1878
(907) 465-2800
http://www.eed.state.ak.us

Substitute teachers are in short supply and high demand. Minimum requirements vary by school district. New subs must be approved by the board of education.

Arizona

Arizona Department of Education
1535 West Jefferson Street
Phoenix, AZ 85007
(800) 352-4558
http://www.ade.state.az.us

A new sub with a bachelor's degree may apply for a Substitute Certificate, which is valid for six years and may be renewed. Official college transcripts and a valid fingerprint clearance card are required. A new sub without a bachelor's degree, but with a high school diploma or GED, may apply for an Emergency Substitute Certificate, which is valid for one school year. The Emergency Substitute Certificate may be renewed with transcripts showing that the applicant has completed at least two semester hours of academic coursework since the previous year's application.

Arkansas

Arkansas Department of Education
4 Capitol Mall
Little Rock, AR 72201
(501) 682-4475
http://arkansased.org

The minimum state requirement for subs is a high school diploma, but other requirements vary by school district.

California

California Department of Education
1430 N Street
Sacramento, CA 95814
(916) 319-0800
http://www.cde.ca.gov
See also: California Commission on Teacher Credentialing

Mailing address:
P.O. Box 944270
Sacramento, CA 94244-2700
http://www.ctc.ca.gov

Physical address:
1900 Capitol Avenue
Sacramento, CA 95814
(888) 921-2682

A bachelor's degree, a passing score on the California Basic Educational Skills Test (CBEST), and fingerprints are required for all substitute teachers. The California Commission on Teacher Credentialing issues the 30-Day Emergency Substitute Teaching Permit for short-term substitutes, which is valid for one year and is renewable. This permit allows subs to work for no more than 30 days in the same regular classroom, and no more than 20 days in the same special education classroom. Long-term subs must be enrolled in a teacher credentialing program at a college or university.

Colorado

Colorado Department of Education
State Office Building
201 East Colfax Avenue
Denver, CO 80203-1799
(303) 866-6600
http://www.cde.state.co.us

A high school diploma or the equivalent thereof, five years of experience in the area to be taught, a vocational credential (issued by the State Board of Education), and participation in a one-year vocational teacher program are required for an Alternative Vocational Teacher License. This license is nonrenewable, but applicants may reapply. Three-year licenses are available to applicants who hold bachelor's degrees, submit fingerprints, pass the Colorado basic skills assessment (PLACE) and oral English proficiency exam, and hold an alternative teacher license. Five-year licenses are available to applicants who meet all of the above requirements and hold or have previously held a valid license.

Connecticut

Connecticut State Department of Education
165 Capitol Avenue
Hartford, CT 06145
(860) 713-6548
http://www.sde.ct.gov

State guidelines require substitute teachers to have a minimum of a bachelor's degree. If a sub spends more than 40 days in the same assignment, the school district must apply for authorization through the Bureau of Certification and Professional Development. An applicant without a bachelor's degree, but who is at least 18 years old and a high school graduate, may obtain an Emergency/Special Circumstances license to substitute teach for up to 40 days in the same assignment. A background check and experience with children are also required.

Delaware

Delaware Department of Education
Main Office:
John G. Townsend Building
401 Federal Street, Suite 2
Dover, DE 19901-3639

Auxiliary Office:
John W. Collette Education Resource Center
35 Commerce Way, Suite 1
Dover, DE 19904-8228
(302) 735-4000
http://www.doe.state.de.us

For a Class A Permit, an applicant must hold a bachelor's degree and either hold or be eligible to hold a standard Delaware teacher's license. For Class B, C, and D Permits, minimum requirements vary by school district.

District of Columbia

District of Columbia Public Schools
Union Square
825 North Capitol Street, NE
Washington, DC 20002
(202) 724-4222
http://www.k12.dc.us

All new subs must submit to fingerprinting and background checks. An applicant with a bachelor's degree may apply for a Full Term Substitute License. An applicant without a bachelor's degree, but who has completed at least 60 semester hours of coursework at an accredited institution, may apply for a Limited Term Substitute License. Both licenses are valid for two years and are renewable.

Federal Schools

(Department of Defense Dependents' Schools)
Policies, procedures, and locations vary. More information is available at http://www.dodea.edu.

Florida

Florida Department of Education
Turlington Building
Suite 1514
325 West Gaines Street
Tallahassee, FL 32399-0400
(850) 245-0505
http://www.fldoe.org

Minimum requirements vary by school district.

Georgia

Georgia Department of Education
2054 Twin Towers East
205 Jesse Hill Jr. Drive SE
Atlanta, GA 30334
(404) 656-2800 or (800) 311-3627
http://www.doe.k12.ga.us

Substitute teachers must have a minimum of a high school diploma or GED. Other requirements vary by district. However, a sub with only a high school diploma or GED may not work for more than 10 consecutive school days. Priority is given to subs with the highest qualifications.

Hawaii

Hawaii Department of Education
Planning and Evaluation
Room 411
1390 Miller Street
Honolulu, HI 96813
(808) 586-3283
http://doe.k12.hi.us
See also: http://tseas.hidoe.us

The state is one large school district, which is divided into geographic units. Each unit is responsible for maintaining a substitute teacher pool. Three classes of substitute teacher licenses are available. For a

Class I license, a sub does not need a bachelor's degree, but must meet Department of Education requirements. Renewal is contingent on successful completion of a 30-hour substitute teacher training course. For a Class II license, which is renewable, a sub must have a bachelor's degree, complete a 30-hour substitute teacher training course, submit to fingerprinting and a background check, and be interviewed. For a Class III license, a sub must be licensed to teach in Hawaii or have successfully completed a state-approved teacher education program. The substitute teacher training course is required for renewal. All licenses are valid for a period of five years.

Idaho

Idaho State Department of Education
650 West State Street
P.O. Box 83720
Boise, ID 83720-0027
(800) 432-4601
http://www.sde.state.id.us/Dept

Minimum requirements vary by school district. Background checks and fingerprinting are required.

Illinois

Illinois State Board of Education
100 North 1st Street
Springfield, IL 62777
(866) 262-6663
100 West Randolph, Suite 14-300
Chicago, IL 60601
(312) 814-2220
http://www.isbe.state.il.us

State guidelines require substitute teachers to have a minimum of a bachelor's degree, or two years of experience and 60 semester hours of coursework in the field of education from a recognized institution of higher learning. Prospective subs may apply for a Substitute Certificate, which is valid for four years and is nonrenewable, but subs may reapply.

Indiana

Indiana Department of Education
State House, Room 229
Indianapolis, IN 46204-2795
(317) 232-6610
http://www.doe.state.in.us

Minimum requirements vary by school district, but a criminal background check is required. The Substitute Teaching Permit is valid for three years.

Iowa

Iowa Department of Education
Grimes State Office Building
East 14th and Grand Streets
Des Moines, IA 50319-0146
(515) 281-3436
http://www.iowa.gov/educate

All subs are required to hold a bachelor's degree and submit to fingerprinting and background checks. A sub who holds a regular teaching certificate may apply for a Substitute Teaching License, which is valid for five years and is renewable, and may spend up to 90 days in the same teaching assignment. A sub who does not hold a regular teaching certificate must complete a substitute teacher training program and then may apply for a Substitute Teacher Authorization, which is valid for one year.

Kansas

Kansas Department of Education
120 Southeast 10th Avenue
Topeka, KS 66612-1182
(785) 296-3201
http://www.ksde.org

A bachelor's degree and completion of a teacher education program is required for the Standard Substitute Certificate; 60 semester hours of coursework from an accredited institution are required for the Emergency Substitute Certificate. Completed fingerprint cards and background checks are required for all subs. The certificates are valid for five years and one year, respectively, and are renewable pending additional requirements.

Kentucky

Kentucky Department of Education
1st Floor, Capital Plaza Tower
500 Mero Street
Frankfort, KY 40601
(502) 564-3421
(800) 533-5372 (KY residents only)
http://www.education.ky.gov/KDE

A prospective sub with a bachelor's degree may apply for a Standard Substitute Certificate, which is valid for five years; it is issued by the state and is renewable upon school district recommendation. A sub without a bachelor's degree may apply for Emergency Certification, which is valid for one year; it is issued by the districts and is nonrenewable (but subs may reapply).

Louisiana

Louisiana Department of Education
Mailing Address:
P.O. Box 94064
Baton Rouge, LA 70804-9064

Physical Address:
Claiborne Building
1201 North 3rd Street
Baton Rouge, LA 70802-5243
(877) 453-2721
http://www.doe.state.la.us

Certified teachers and substitutes are in short supply, and minimum requirements vary by parish. Some schools offer incentives to attract highly qualified substitutes.

Maine

Maine Department of Education
Burton M. Cross State Office Building
111 Sewall Street
Augusta, ME
(207) 624-6600
http://www.maine.gov/education

Substitute teachers do not need a bachelor's degree, but requirements vary by school district. Applicants must be fingerprinted and submit to a criminal record check.

Maryland

Maryland Department of Education
200 West Baltimore Street
Baltimore, MD 21201
(410) 767-0100
http://www.marylandpublicschools.org/msde

Minimum requirements vary by school district.

Massachusetts

Massachusetts Department of Education
350 Main Street
Malden, MA 02148
(781) 338-3000
http://www.doe.mass.edu

Minimum requirements vary by school district.

Michigan

Michigan Department of Education
608 West Allegan Street
P.O. Box 30008
Lansing, MI 48909
(517) 373-3324
http://www.michigan.gov/mde

Prospective subs need to complete at least 90 hours of coursework at an accredited four-year college or university and apply to local school districts for a Substitute Permit, which is valid for one school year (150 days) and is renewable. A background check is required.

Minnesota

Minnesota Department of Education
1500 Highway 36 West
Roseville, MN 55113-4266
(651) 582-8200
http://education.state.mn.us

All subs are required to hold a bachelor's degree, be fingerprinted, and submit to a background check. The state issues three different types of substitute teaching licenses. The Limited Short Call License requires a bachelor's degree in any subject; the sub cannot work for more than 15 consecutive days. The Standard Short Call and Substitute Licenses require a bachelor's degree in education as well as other qualifications and are valid for five years. All are renewable.

Mississippi

Mississippi Department of Education
Central High School
P.O. Box 771
359 North West Street
Jackson, MS 39205
(601) 359-3513
http://www.mde.k12.ms.us

Minimum requirements vary by school district.

Missouri

Missouri Department of Elementary and Secondary Education
P.O. Box 480
Jefferson City, MO 65102
(573) 751-4212
http://dese.mo.gov

For a permit valid for 45 days, a sub must have completed 60–119 semester units of university credit. For a 90-day permit, a sub must have completed at least 120 semester units of university credit. For a Substitute Certificate, which is valid for one school year, a sub must have completed at least 60 semester hours of university credit and apply directly to a school district. Other qualifications may apply. All certificates are nonrenewable; subs must reapply.

Montana

Montana Office of Public Instruction
P.O. Box 202501
Helena, MT 59620-2501
(406) 444-2082
http://www.opi.mt.gov

Local school districts hire their own substitute teachers, so requirements vary by district. Long-term subs who work in the same assignment for more than 30 days must be certified.

Nebraska

Nebraska Department of Education
301 Centennial Mall South
Lincoln, NE 68509
(402) 471-2295
http://www.nde.state.ne.us

Every sub must complete Human Relations Training and have a fingerprint clearance card (if they have not been a Nebraska resident for five consecutive years). A prospective sub without a bachelor's degree, but with at least 60 semester units of university credit, one semester of professional education, and at least one course in multicultural studies, may apply for a Local Substitute Teaching Certificate, which permits 40 days of subbing each year for three years and is renewable. A prospective sub who has completed a bachelor's degree, Human Relations Training, and a teacher training program, and who holds regular teaching certification in Nebraska or another state, may apply for a Substitute Teaching License, which is valid for five years and is renewable pending 50 days of teaching or three semester hours of preapproved college credit.

Nevada

Nevada Department of Education
700 East Fifth Street
Carson City, NV 89701
(775) 687-9141
http://www.doe.nv.gov

The State Department of Education issues the Substitute License and requires subs to have a minimum of either a bachelor's degree or 62 semester hours of college credit, including six semester credits in education. The license is valid for three years.

New Hampshire

New Hampshire Department of Education
101 Pleasant Street
Concord, NH 03301-3860
(603) 271-3494
http://www.ed.state.nh.us/education

Subs are in short supply and are usually hired by individual school districts. Minimum requirements vary by district. A sub working in the same assignment for more than 20 days must be certified in the subject being taught.

New Jersey

New Jersey Department of Education
P.O. Box 500
Trenton, NJ 08625
(609) 292-4469
http://www.state.nj.us/education

Under the New Jersey Administrative Code, applicants who complete at least 60 semester hours of course credit at an accredited college can apply for a certificate to substitute teach in a particular county. Subs are limited to 20 consecutive days in the same assignment. The certificate is valid for three years.

New Mexico

New Mexico Public Education Department
300 Don Gaspar
Santa Fe, NM 87501-2786
(505) 827-5800
http://www.sde.state.nm.us

Substitute teachers must be over the age of 18 to teach Grades K–8, and over 21 years of age to teach Grades 9–12. All must have a high school diploma or the equivalent thereof. School districts approve a list of prospective substitutes, who can then be licensed for up to three years. The Substitute Teacher License is renewable.

New York

New York State Education Department
Education Building
Room 111
89 Washington Avenue
Albany, NY 12234
(518) 474-3852
http://www.nysed.gov

Minimum requirements vary by school district. Some districts may hire permanent substitutes.

North Carolina

North Carolina Department of Public Instruction
301 North Wilmington Street
Raleigh, NC 27601
(919) 807-3300
http://www.ncpublicschools.org

Minimum requirements vary by school district. Some districts may hire full-time substitutes.

North Dakota

North Dakota Department of Public Instruction
Department 201
600 East Boulevard Avenue
Bismarck, ND 58505-0440
(701) 328-2260
http://www.dpi.state.nd.us

Fingerprints and a bachelor's degree are required. Substitutes must hold a valid certificate issued by the state Department of Public Instruction. This certification is valid for two years and is renewable. An emergency substitute must have a bachelor's degree in the content area of instruction. This certification is valid for one year and is renewable.

Ohio

Ohio Department of Education
25 South Front Street
Columbus, OH 43215-4183
(614) 466 4839
(877) 644-6338
http://www.ode.state.oh.us

All subs must have a bachelor's degree. Short-term subs may teach fewer than five consecutive days in the same assignment. Long-term subs may teach more than five consecutive days in the same assignment, and must have completed 12 semester hours of early childhood education coursework and 20 semester hours of coursework in each subject to be taught. Each permit is valid for one or five years and may be renewed upon recommendation of the district superintendent. Some school districts hire full-time substitutes.

Oklahoma

Oklahoma State Department of Education
2500 North Lincoln Boulevard
Oklahoma City, OK 73105
(405) 521-3977 (Human Resources)
http://www.sde.state.ok.us

Minimum requirements vary by school district.

Oregon

Oregon Department of Education
255 Capitol Street NE
Salem, OR 97310-0203
(503) 378-3569
http://www.ode.state.or.us

A substitute must hold a bachelor's degree and obtain a license issued by the state Teacher Standards and Practices Commission. To obtain a Substitute License, an applicant must hold a teaching certificate and a bachelor's degree in the content area to be taught, and must pass a test of verbal skills, computational skills, and civil rights laws. An applicant without a teaching certificate may apply for a Restricted Substitute License after passing a test of verbal skills, computational skills, and civil rights laws. Both licenses are valid for three years and are renewable.

Pennsylvania

Pennsylvania Department of Education
333 Market Street
Harrisburg, PA 17126-0333
(717) 783-6788
http://www.pde.state.pa.us

An Emergency Substitute must have a bachelor's degree, whereas a Certified Substitute must have both a bachelor's degree and a teaching certificate. Also, each sub must have a background check, fingerprinting, Pennsylvania Child Abuse Clearance History, recent TB/Tine test, three professional letters of reference, and two forms of identification. Both forms of substitute teacher certification are valid for one year and are renewable.

Rhode Island

Rhode Island Department of Elementary and Secondary Education
255 Westminster Street
Providence, RI 02903-3400
(401) 222-4600
http://www.ridoe.net

All subs must hold a bachelor's degree. A Certified Substitute must also hold a teaching certificate. An Emergency Substitute must have a bachelor's degree in the subject area to be taught. Emergency subs may only be hired if no Certified subs are available.

South Carolina

South Carolina Department of Education
1006 Rutledge Building
1429 Senate Street
Columbia, SC 29201
(803) 734-8493
http://www.ed.sc.gov

Minimum requirements vary by school district. Some districts offer orientation programs to new subs before they begin to work in classrooms.

South Dakota

South Dakota Department of Education
700 Governors Drive
Pierre, SD 57501-2291
(605) 773-3553
http://doe.sd.gov

Minimum requirements vary by school district.

Tennessee

Tennessee Department of Education
Andrew Johnson Tower, 6th Floor
Nashville, TN 37243-0375
(615) 741-2731
http://www.state.tn.us/education

Minimum requirements vary by school district. Some districts provide professional development sessions and training for substitutes.

Texas

Texas Education Agency
William Travis Building
1701 North Congress Avenue
Austin, TX 78701
(512) 463-9734
http://www.tea.state.tx.us

The state education system is divided into regions. Minimum requirements vary.

Utah

State of Utah Office of Education
P.O. Box 144200
250 East 500 South
Salt Lake City, UT 84114-4200
(801) 538-7500
http://www.schools.utah.gov

A prospective sub must be a high school graduate and may not work in the same assignment for more than eight weeks. Other requirements vary by school district.

Vermont

Vermont Department of Education
120 State Street
Montpelier, VT 05620-2501
(802) 828-2445 (Licensing)
(802) 828-0584 (Human Resources)
http://education.vermont.gov/

A prospective sub must be a high school graduate and may not work in the same assignment for more than 15 consecutive days. Other requirements vary by school district.

Virginia

Virginia Department of Education
P.O. Box 2120
Richmond, VA 23218
(800) 292-3820
http://www.pen.k12.va.us

Subs must be at least 18 years old, have a high school diploma or the equivalent thereof, and attend an orientation. Training and credentials vary across the state, with some school districts requiring higher credentials than the state-mandated minimum qualifications.

Washington

Office of the Superintendent of Public Instruction
Old Capitol Building
600 South Washington
P.O. Box 47200
Olympia, WA 98504-7200
(360) 725-6000
http://www.k12.wa.us

A Regular Substitute (valid indefinitely) must have a bachelor's degree and a teaching certificate. Fingerprinting is required if the teaching certificate is not from Washington. An Emergency Substitute (valid for up to three years and renewable) need not have a bachelor's degree or teaching certificate. Other requirements may apply.

West Virginia

West Virginia Department of Education
1900 Kanawha Boulevard East
Charleston, WV 25305
(304) 558-2389 (Office of Personnel Development)
http://wvde.state.wv.us

Prospective substitute teachers can apply to the state Department of Education for Short-Term and Long-Term Permits. A Short-Term sub must have completed a bachelor's degree from an accredited college or university with a minimum 2.0 grade point average. This permit is valid for three years and is renewable. A Long-Term sub must have completed a bachelor's degree from an accredited college or university with a minimum 2.0 grade point average, and have completed at least 12 semester units of coursework in the content area to be taught. This permit is valid for three years and is renewable pending completion of in-service hours. All subs must also be fingerprinted. Other requirements may apply.

Wisconsin

Wisconsin Department of Public Instruction
125 South Webster Street
P.O. Box 7841
Madison, WI 53707-7841
(800) 441-4563
http://dpi.wi.gov

The Wisconsin Department of Public Instruction grants a renewable three-year Substitute Teacher Permit to prospective subs who hold a bachelor's degree from an accredited institution but who have not completed a state-approved educator preparation program. Permit holders can work in the same assignment for up to 20 consecutive days. Applicants with a bachelor's degree and a teaching certificate may apply for the renewable five-year Substitute Teacher License, which permits long-term subbing assignments.

Wyoming

Wyoming Department of Education
Hathaway Building
Second Floor
2300 Capitol Avenue
Cheyenne, WY 82002-0050
(307) 777-7675
http://www.k12.wy.us

Subs are not required to hold a bachelor's degree, but a prospective sub must have completed 65 semester hours of college credit as well as 24 hours of in-service (10 of which must be spent in observation), pass a United States/Wyoming constitution course or equivalency test, and submit a set of fingerprints for a background check to qualify for a Sub Permit. The permit is valid for five years and is renewable pending professional development workshop hours.

Resource B: Substitute Teacher's Log

Copy this chart as many times as necessary, and use it to record each of your substitute teaching jobs. In a short time, you will have developed a reference list that you can consult when asked to return to a school or class.

Date	*School*	*Times*	*Teacher*	*Grades/Subjects*	*Notes*

Resource C: Elementary School Sub Report

Date: ______________________

Regular Teacher: _______________________

Hello! My name is ___________________________________ and I substitute taught your class today. If you have any questions, please feel free to contact me at this number: _________________.

Notes regarding lesson plans and material covered:

In addition to the lesson plan, we also did the following:

Behavior and classroom management notes:

Other notes or information:

The following students were absent from class today:

Resource D: Secondary School Sub Report

Date: ___________________

Regular Teacher: ________________________

Hello! My name is _____________________________________ and I substitute taught your classes today. If you have any questions, please feel free to contact me at this number: __________________.

Class	*Lesson Content Covered*	*Student Behavior Notes*
1		
2		
3		
4		
5		
6		
7		
8		

Other notes or information:

Resource E: Online Sources of Free Materials for Teachers and Substitutes

The Internet is positively bursting with downloadable, printable, and ready-to-use lesson plans and activities, many of which are free of charge. As a substitute teacher, you can find materials for any grade level and any subject. The Internet is ever changing, and online communities come and go. However, I have visited all of the Web sites below, and all were still being maintained as of October 2007.

Dave's ESL Café: The Internet's Meeting Place for ESL and EFL Teachers and Students From Around the World
http://www.eslcafe.com
This site offers a message board and countless lessons and activities for teaching English language learners.

Education World: The Educator's Best Friend
http://www.educationworld.com
This site offers lesson plans, activities, professional development resources, and more.

Houghton Mifflin Education Place
http://www.eduplace.com
Use the *Activity Search* button to find PreK–6 resources for teachers, students, and parents.

National Substitute Teachers Alliance (NSTA)
http://www.nstasubs.org
This site has plentiful resources, tips, links, a chat board, and more. It also posts information about NSTA membership and annual conferences.

ProTeacher Community
http://www.proteacher.net
This is an online community of educators and includes a message board.

The Substitute Teacher: Puzzles and Other Diversions
http://www.subhelp.com
This site contains printable puzzles and games that substitute teachers can use to fill up extra class time.

Substitute Teacher Homepage: The Substitute Teacher Survival Site
http://www.csrnet.org/csrnet/substitute
This site offers activities, lesson plans, suggestions, and tips for subs.

Teachers.net: The Ultimate Teacher Resource
http://teachers.net
This site provides ready-made lessons, activities, message boards, and morc.

TeacherVision
http://www.teachervision.fen.com
This site provides complete lesson plans, K–8 stand-alone units, and other resources.

Glossary

Administrator. A person who works within the school system to organize, manage, and facilitate the education process. Examples include school principals, assistant principals, deans, and superintendents.

Adult school. See *school for adults.*

Advanced placement (AP). Courses specifically designed to prepare college-bound high school students to take standardized subject-specific tests. AP courses include English, Biology, and Chemistry. Not all schools offer all AP courses.

Anecdotal records. Notes or a journal that you maintain to record events that take place during your workday.

Bilingual education. School programs in which limited-English-proficient students receive temporary language assistance as they learn to function in an English-speaking academic environment.

Block schedule. Schedule in which students attend half of their classes on certain days of the week, and their other classes on the other days of the week. Each class lasts for approximately two hours, or the equivalent of two regular class periods.

Classroom management. What a teacher does to direct what happens in a classroom.

Continuation high school. Schools designed to support the needs of students who have dropped out of or been expelled from regular high schools in the district. Often, this is their last opportunity to earn a high school diploma.

Department of Defense Dependents' school. See *Department of Defense Education Activity.*

Department of Defense Education Activity. Schools on American military bases are overseen by the Department of Defense Education Activity (DoDEA). DoDEA's schools serve the children of military service members and Department of Defense civilian employees throughout the world. DoDEA operates public schools in the United States and overseas. Such schools are sometimes referred to as Federal Schools or Department of Defense Dependents' Schools.

Educational Testing Service (ETS). A nonprofit organization that develops and administers standardized assessment tools for a wide variety of educational purposes. More information can be found at www.ets.org.

Elementary school. A school usually attended by students in kindergarten through sixth grade.

English as a second language (ESL). Classes designed to teach English to speakers of other languages. English is not necessarily the learners' second language, but may be a third, fourth, or fifth.

Extended-term sub. See *long-term sub.*

Faculty. Teachers, professors, and other school employees who teach students.

Faculty relations. Professional connections and relationships with your colleagues.

Federal school. See *Department of Defense Education Activity.*

Fire drill. A situation in which everyone on the school campus practices what they must do in the event of a real fire.

Full-time sub. A substitute teacher who reports for work every day to a designated school site and fills in for absent teachers as needed. Full-time subs may help with administrative duties or assist in other ways when no teachers are absent.

Gifted and talented education (GATE). Special programs designed to challenge academically gifted learners.

High school. School for students in Grades 9–12, but sometimes only for Grades 10–12.

Independent study. Work performed or material studied outside of an organized class, for which students receive academic credit; usually supervised by a teacher.

Intern teacher. A full-time teacher who is concurrently in the process of completing the requirements for his or her teaching license or credential.

Junior high school. School for students in Grades 7–9.

K–8 school. School for students in kindergarten through eighth grade.

K–12 school. School for students in kindergarten through twelfth grade.

Lesson plan. A document that lists the goals, procedures, timelines, and any other important information regarding the delivery of a lesson; the amount of detail may vary widely.

Local basic administrative unit. See *school district.*

Local education agency. See *school district.*

Long-term sub. A substitute teacher who fills in for the same regular teacher for an extended period of time. The minimum length of time for a long-term assignment varies by state, and sometimes by district, but is often about 15 days.

Middle school. A school for students in the seventh and eighth grades. Serves as a bridge between elementary school and high school.

Networking. The process of developing contacts and building professional working relationships with colleagues.

Newcomer school. A school that serves the needs of learners who have recently immigrated to the United States and are acclimatizing socially and developing their English language skills.

On task. Actively engaged in the learning process and/or the task at hand.

Payroll. A list of employees and their pay information. This term is often used to refer to the school district department in charge of processing paychecks.

Permanent teacher. See *regular teacher.*

Primary school. A school for students in kindergarten through third grade.

Private school. A school that is not controlled by a government entity, but rather by an individual or an agency. Funding comes from tuition and private sources instead of public funds.

Public school. A school that is controlled by a government entity and is financed by public funds.

Regular teacher. The instructor who usually teaches a class.

Safe Schools Policy. A policy in place in most school districts to ensure a safe environment for students, faculty, staff, visitors, and neighbors.

School district. A local education agency that operates public schools within a given geographic area. Synonyms include *local basic administrative unit* and *local education agency.*

School for adults. In addition to high school diplomas and/or GED certificates for students over the age of 18, this type of school frequently also offers ESL and citizenship classes for adult immigrants, parenting classes, computer training, and more for members of the community.

Secondary school. A school for students in any of grades seven through twelve. Middle schools, junior high schools, and high schools are included.

Short-term sub. A substitute teacher who fills in for the regular teacher for a limited period of time. The length of time differs by state but is usually only one or two days, and must be fewer than 15 days or so.

Special education. School programs designed to serve students with exceptional needs.

Staff. School or district support personnel.

Staggered schedule. Schedule in which some students arrive and leave earlier than other students, who arrive and leave later in the day.

Student teacher. A teacher who is in the process of fulfilling licensing/credentialing requirements by teaching for a period of time under the guidance of a master teacher.

Sub pack. A bag of useful supplies that a substitute teacher prepares and brings to school.

Substitute educator. See *substitute teacher.*

Substitute teacher. A school or district employee who temporarily fulfills the duties of an absent regular teacher.

Teacher's license. Certification that a teacher has completed the necessary requirements to teach particular grades and/or subjects.

Teachers union. An organization representing educators and paraprofessionals, dedicated to protecting the quality of education, members' rights, and advocating for fair compensation, benefits, and job security.

Teaching credential. See *teacher's license.*

Traditional school year. School begins in the late summer or early fall, students take a short break in the winter and again in the spring, and then are dismissed for summer vacation.

Year-round school. A school in which, instead of a long break in the summer, students take shorter breaks throughout the calendar year.

Youth authority. A juvenile detention center.

References

Bailey, K. M., B. Bergthold, B. Braunstein, N. J. Fleischman, M. P. Holbrook, J. Tuman, X. Waissbluth, and L. J. Zambo. 1996. The language teacher's autobiography: Examining "the apprenticeship of observation." In *Teacher learning in language teaching*, ed. D. Freeman and J. C. Richards, 11–29. Cambridge: Cambridge University Press.

Banks, J. A. 1994. *Multiethnic education: Theory and practice.* 3rd ed. Boston: Allyn & Bacon.

Boise School District Employment and Application Center. 2006. *Substitute information: Certified and classified.* http://www.boiseschools.org/jobs/substitute.html.

Brown, H. D. 2001. *Teaching by principles: An interactive approach to language pedagogy*. New York: Longman.

California Department of Education. 2006, May 2. *Data and statistics: Report for number of teachers by ethnicity for the years 1981–82 to 2004–05*. http://www.cde.ca.gov/ds/sd/cb/ethteach.asp.

Don't Sweat Press Editors. 2003. *Don't sweat guide for teachers: Cutting through the clutter so that every day counts.* New York: Hyperion.

Gaither, J. 1998. *Survival kit for the substitute and new teacher*. Baltimore: Jenrod.

Gregory, G. H., and Chapman, C. 2007. *Differentiated instructional strategies: One size doesn't fit all.* 2nd ed. Thousand Oaks, CA: Corwin Press.

Kennedy, J. F. 1964. *A nation of immigrants.* New York: Harper & Row.

Kennedy, M. 1990. *Policy issues in teacher education.* East Lansing, MI: National Center for Research on Teacher Learning.

Kohl, H. 1984. *Growing minds: On becoming a teacher.* New York: Harper & Row.

Lortie, D. 1975. *Schoolteacher: A sociological study.* Chicago: University of Chicago Press.

National Education Association. 2002. *Status of substitute teachers: A state-by-state summary.* http://www.nea.org/substitutes/statebystate.html.

———. 2005. *Rankings and estimates: Rankings of the states 2004 and estimates of school statistics 2005*. Washington, DC: NEA Research.

———. 2006. *Substitute educators.* http://www.nea.org/substitutes/index.html.

National Substitute Teachers Alliance. 2003, January 16. *Guest teachers push for respect.* http://www.nstasubs.org/sacramento_bee_1–16–03.htm.

Nieto, S. 2000. *Affirming diversity: The sociopolitical context of multicultural education* 3rd ed. New York: Longman.

NYC Department of Education. 2006, June 9. *Substitutes/per diem.* http://www.nycenet.edu/Offices/DHR/Employees/SubstituteTeachers PerDiem.

Oregon School Boards Association. 2006, April 11. *Human resource development: 2005–2006 substitute teacher pay.* http://www.osba.org/lrelatns/salary/subpay/index.htm.

Schneidewind, N., and Davidson, E. 1998. *Open minds to equality: A sourcebook of learning activities to affirm diversity and promote equity.* Needham Heights, MA: Allyn & Bacon.

Substitute teacher handbook K–12. 6th ed. 2004. Logan, UT: Substitute Teaching Institute/Utah State University.

Substitute Teaching Institute. 2006. *State requirements.* https://sti.usu.edu/common/documents/state_requirements.pdf.

———. 2007. *About STI: Philosophy.* https://sti.usu.edu/subs/aboutsti/philosophy.aspx.

United States Census Bureau. 2000. *Census 2000 redistricting data (PL 94-171) summary file.* http://www.census.gov/prod/www/abs/pl94-171.pdf

Warner, J., and Bryan, C. 2006. *The unauthorized teacher's survival guide.* 3rd ed. Indianapolis, IN: Jist Works.

Wilke, R. L. 2003. *The first days of class: A practical guide for the beginning teacher.* Thousand Oaks, CA: Corwin Press.

Suggested Readings

Materials for Subs

These books contain ready-made lesson plans and activities (some require that you have access to a photocopy machine) for various grade levels and subject areas, activities for filling in that last five or ten minutes of class time, and suggestions for organizing your records and materials.

Dellinger, J. 2006. *The substitute teaching survival guide, grades K–5: Emergency lesson plans and essential advice.* San Francisco: Jossey-Bass.

———. 2005. *The substitute teaching survival guide, grades 6–12: Emergency lesson plans and essential advice.* San Francisco: Jossey-Bass.

Herbst, J. 2001. *The substitute teacher's organizer: A comprehensive resource to make every teaching assignment a success.* Huntington Beach, CA: Creative Teaching.

Nelson, P. 1986. *Teacher's bag of tricks: 101 instant lessons for classroom fun.* Nashville, TN: Incentive.

Schneidewind, N., and Davidson, E. 1998. *Open minds to equality: A sourcebook of learning activities to affirm diversity and promote equity.* Needham Heights, MA: Allyn & Bacon.

Information About Substitute Teaching

These two books contain more information on the general subject of subbing. They are designed for administrators who want to offer training and professional development to their substitute teachers.

Rowley, J. B., and P. M. Hart. 1998. *Recruiting and training successful substitute teachers.* Thousand Oaks, CA: Corwin Press.

St. Michel, T. 1995. *Effective substitute teachers: Myth, mayhem, or magic.* Thousand Oaks, CA: Corwin Press.

Classroom Management

Take a look at these books if you are interested in further developing your knowledge of classroom management methods and exploring your approach to classroom teaching. Most address the issue of developing positive working relationships with your students.

Belvel, P. M., and Jordan, M. M. 2002. *Rethinking classroom management: Strategies for prevention, intervention, and problem solving.* Thousand Oaks: Corwin Press.

Glasser, W. 1990. *The quality school teacher.* New York: HarperCollins.

Halaby, M. 2000. *Creating community in the classroom.* Brookline, MA: Brookline Books.

Kohl, H. 1984. *Growing minds: On becoming a teacher.* New York: Harper & Row.

Lindberg, J. A., D. E. Kelley, and A. M. Swick. 2004. *Common-sense classroom management for middle and high school teachers.* Thousand Oaks, CA: SAGE.

Lindberg, J. A., and A. M. Swick. 2006. *Common-sense classroom management for elementary school tea*chers. Thousand Oaks, CA: SAGE.

Nelsen, J., Lott, L., and Glen, H. S. 1997. *Positive discipline in the classroom.* Rocklin, CA: Prima.

Smith, R. 2004. *Conscious classroom management.* Thousand Oaks, CA: Corwin Press.

Vito, J. M. 2003. *Relationship-driven classroom management: Strategies that promote student motivation.* Thousand Oaks, CA: SAGE.

Warner, J., and Bryan, C. 2006. *The unauthorized teacher's survival guide.* 3rd ed. Indianapolis, IN: Jist Works.

Wilke, R. L. 2003. *The first days of class: A practical guide for the beginning teacher.* Thousand Oaks, CA: Corwin Press.

Teaching Methodology

The books below address specific teaching strategies and methodologies.

Brown, H. D. 2001. *Teaching by principles: An interactive approach to language pedagogy.* New York: Longman.

Gregory, G. H., and Chapman, C. 2007. *Differentiated instructional strategies: One size doesn't fit all.* 2nd ed. Thousand Oaks, CA: Corwin Press.

Larimer, R., and L. Schleicher, eds. 1999. *New ways in using authentic materials in the classroom.* Alexandria, VA: Teachers of English to Speakers of Other Languages.

Index

The Corwin Press logo—a raven striding across an open book—represents the union of courage and learning. Corwin Press is committed to improving education for all learners by publishing books and other professional development resources for those serving the field of PreK–12 education. By providing practical, hands-on materials, Corwin Press continues to carry out the promise of its motto: **"Helping Educators Do Their Work Better."**